The Christchurch Cookery Book

A thousand years of food in Christchurch

© Natula Publications 2000

ISBN 1 897 887 24 8

Published by Natula Publications
5 St Margaret's Avenue, Christchurch Dorset BH23 1JD

British Library Cataloguing-in-Publication Data
A catalogue record for this book is available from the British Library

Publishers Note: The recipes that have been submitted for inclusion in this book have been accepted in good faith. Whilst every effort has been made to check and verify them, not all of the recipes have been tested by being fully prepared and cooked. The publishers are therefore unable to accept responsibility for the total accuracy of the recipes.

Celebrity Chefs pictured on the front cover : (from left to right)

James Martin
Chocolate and Ginger Cheesecake (page 121)

Lesley Waters
Cheese and Apple Scofa Bread (page 158)

Ken Hom
Steamed Salmon with Black Beans (page 45)

Marguerite Patten
Chicken with Pine Nuts and Red Pepper (page 69)

Patrick Anthony
Raspberry Tart/Fruit and Almond Tart (pages 122,123)

Anton Edelmann
Pear with Chocolate and Amaretto Sabayon (page 124)

Mary Berry
Whole Orange Spice Cake (page 157)

Cover Illustrations:
Photographs of Christchurch Harbour and Place Mill taken by David Bailey

Introduction

Anton Edelmann
Maître Chef des Cuisines
The Savoy Hotel, London

The Millennium is a time to look back and take stock as well as looking forward to the future. Therefore it was suggested that a book should be produced in conjunction with the Food and Wine Festival as part of the Millennium celebrations in Christchurch which would reflect a thousand years of food and cooking in this area as well as including current recipes.

The recipes in the Christchurch Cookery Book have been submitted by organisations based in the town or by individuals who either live or work within the Borough of Christchurch. They reflect the diversity of food on offer in our many restaurants, hotels and guest houses and the enormous choice of foods available from the town's supermarkets and specialist food shops. The book also contains traditional dishes which have been cooked in this area for generations and these can be found among recipes for continental dishes, Chinese, Indian and South African food. There is a chapter on vegetarian food, a comparatively recent trend, as well as sections on fish and game which have been mainstays of Christchurch cooking for centuries.

I was delighted to be asked to be the President of the Christchurch Food and Wine Festival and to provide a recipe for this book which is included together with those from the other celebrity chefs Patrick Anthony, Mary Berry, Ken Hom, James Martin, Marguerite Patten, and Lesley Waters who are also participating in the Festival.

Join with us in celebrating 1,000 years of cooking in Christchurch.

Take a stroll back through time and find out about the food eaten in this area over the centuries. Browse through the many recipes and discover the wide range of food cooked in Christchurch today. Let the recipes stimulate your taste buds and try out some of them yourself. Share in the obvious interest in cooking here and above all enjoy your food.

Remember the old proverb:

"The table attracts more friends than the mind."

Acknowledgements

There are many people to thank for helping with the production of this book as it really was a community effort. Firstly we would like to thank all of the people and organisations who submitted recipes to be included in the book because without them there would not have been a book. The response was overwhelming and we were unable to publish every recipe we received. We apologise to anyone we have left out but we did try to involve as many people as we could.

Many people gave up their time to help or offered advice for which we are very grateful. In particular we would like to thank Yas Maybank for typing the initial batch of recipes; Susan Eckstein FICSc for checking through numerous recipes and answering our many culinary queries and Mary Reader FICSc for launching the idea and providing the initial ground work.

The staff at the Red House Museum, especially Jim Hunter and Linda Arnold, gave valuable assistance with the history of food in the area as did Ken Tullett, Archivist at Christchurch Priory; Mike Allen at Highcliffe Castle; Michael Hodges, Betty Peters, Michael Stannard and Olive Samuel from Christchurch Local History Society and Pat Judge at Highcliffe Local History Society, for which we are very grateful. We would also like to thank John Lewis and Sally Glennie for allowing us to use their illustrations and sharing with us a wealth of information from their knowledge of and interest in the local area.

We would also like to thank Julian White for his help with the design and Mike and Ann Hyde of Bookends for their advice on the production of the book.

We are pleased to be able to include recipes by the celebrity chefs and would thank their respective agents and publishers for allowing this.

Jane Martin
Natula Publications

Contents

Coloured Illustrations

History of Food in Christchurch

Food and its cooking has a long and varied history in Christchurch. Throughout the centuries the fashions have been followed firstly by the lords of the manors, the nobles and the gentry, copying the cuisine of the royal courts and then by the aspiring middle classes especially with the general availability and popularity of cookery books. Nowadays we have a wealth of books on food. With the advent of television and computers, coupled with the fact that schools teach cookery to boys as well as girls, existing cooking techniques and new ideas and trends in food are available to everybody.

It is known that this area was inhabited in prehistoric times. The Reindeer Hunters, with their bone and antler tools lived on Hengistbury Head over 125,000 years ago. Stone Age man, on Hengistbury Head, used a primitive form of cooking with stone pot boilers. We know too, from excavations, that there was an Iron Age port on the edge of Christchurch Harbour importing wine from the continent and that the Romans were in occupation about 2,000 years ago. But we shall consider the history of cooking in Christchurch to begin with the birth of the town itself around Christchurch Priory.

Sweet Wine Cakes *from* ***Highcliffe Local History Society*** *for their Roman evening.*

450g (1 lb) self-raising flour	*60g (2 oz) lard*
1 tablespoon sweet white wine	*30g (1 oz) cheese, grated*
pinch aniseed	*1 egg (beaten)*
pinch cumin	*12 bay leaves*

Pre-heat the oven to 200°C/400°F/Gas 6.

Moisten the flour with the wine and add the aniseed and cumin. Rub in the lard and grated cheese and bind the mixture with the egg and a little milk if required.

Shape into 12 small cakes and place each one on a bay leaf. Bake in the oven for 20 to 25 minutes.

Christchurch, then named Twynham, was an early Christian settlement which prospered and grew. In the 9th century it had a royal burgh status and by late Norman times the town's name was changing to that of its greatest building Christ's church. The Augustinian Priory with its conventual buildings became a centre of pilgrimage which encouraged trade and the town continued to flourish. The Priory would have had large kitchens to cook the food for all the canons and a separate building housed the bakery. Bread was a vital part of the diet. Place Mill would have been used, since Saxon times, to grind corn into flour.

The diet of labourers living in Christchurch changed little over the centuries. It consisted mainly of bread, cheese, potato (since 16th century) and pottage (broth). During the Medieval period stale bread was used for plates. This was gradually replaced by wooden trenchers. Ale, beer and cider were drunk though in later centuries tea became more popular. A document lists the provision of food given in the workhouse (now the Red House Museum) to the inmates in 1812. It shows that breakfast consisted of broth; supper was always bread, cheese and beer. Dinner varied only slightly, examples being beef served with bread, bacon and potatoes and pease broth. On two days during the week dinner con-

-sisted of bread, cheese and beer. Meat alternatives of mutton and veal and fish were used to vary the food from week to week. The inmates had to work for their food and lodgings. The standard of living inside the workhouse, which took in the destitute, differed little from life outside the workhouse for most people.

The upper classes and gentry have always had an abundance of food. Farmers normally fared well but their food changed little over the centuries. Home produced milk, cream, butter and eggs with which to cook, home-baked bread and home-cured ham and bacon hanging from large hooks in the ceiling of the farmhouse kitchen were not uncommon sights in the centre of Christchurch until last century. Cooking would have been done over an open fire or in a range. The building that houses Castles, the iron mongers, in Bargates was Home Farm until 1923. The shop still has the old stone floor. Another farm which existed in the centre of Christchurch until comparatively recently was McArdle's farm in Wick Lane. During the Second World War the ground was used for the 'Dig for Victory' campaign. At the end of the war the Wickfield Estate was built on this land. The Borough is gradually losing its farms. However, some farmhouses still remain and a few of them are of considerable age such as Grove Farm and Staple Cross Farm which date from medieval times and Bosley Farm at Hurn which is reputed to be even older.

Since the earliest times the whole town would have joined in with the feasting and merrymaking during the two annual fairs, both of which continued until the late 19th century. The Borough Fair was held on St. Faith's Day (October 17th) and the Trinity Fair took place in June on Corpus Christi Day. A whole ox would have been roasted over a spit in the market square and much ale or beer would have been drunk.

Beer has always been brewed in Christchurch from the time of the Augustinian Priory until recently when a special beer 'Priory Gold' was produced by Cooks Brewery for the 900th anniversary of Christchurch Priory in 1994. The 19th century was the period which boasted the largest number of breweries - no fewer than 9 - and therefore there was a profusion of places in which to imbibe. By the middle of that century there were 26 inns and 16 beer houses! Christchurch still has a good number of pubs, many predate the Victorian period and some are considerably older. Beer would undoubtedly have been added to dishes, and some local licensed premises serving food continue to do so as can be seen from the recipes.

Everybody would have celebrated the saints days and feast days such as the Harvest Home and Christmas. Christmas cakes and puddings would have been made and wassail, from the Anglo-Saxon for good health, a drink made with apples and similar to mulled wine would have been drunk at this time. Easter and Lent were known for their special foods: Easter eggs; pancakes for Shrove Tuesday (to use up any meat and dairy produce before the start of Lent); furmenty (a thick broth made from wheat) and kedgeree on Good Friday. Traditionally hot cross buns were made throughout Lent. The meatless days of Lent and the eating of fish on a Friday date back to the Roman Catholic faith in the time before Henry VIII. When people began drifting away from Catholicism in the mid 1500s, legislation was brought in to make Fridays meatless in order to help our then ailing fishing industry. It is interesting to note how many of the above customs still survive.

To the lords of the manor and the gentry food was more than a necessity; entertaining was important and they would have followed the fashions in cuisine. From the beginning, being a royal burgh, the monarch would have visited Christchurch and the lord of the manor would have had to produce a banquet fit enough for a king. Indeed there were times when the lord of the manor was a king or queen. Henry I and Edward I both held this position. One can imagine, inside the castle complex, the large hall with long tables laden with various dishes; the central table elaborately decorated with perhaps a swan dressed up as the centre piece, complete with feathers. The food was very visual. As well as being spiced (this masked the flavour of salted meat), it was highly scented and coloured. Flowers, such as violets, were used for decoration and jellies set in different coloured layers were popular. Saffron and parsley, two of the many natural dyes were used to colour dishes yellow and green respectively. Syrup of violets would colour food purple and beetroot juice provided a red dye. Delicacies, gifts or food for a special guest were gilded using real gold. The tableware of nobles' households would also have been made of gold.

The Crusaders, returning from the Holy Land, brought back new foods with them such as different spices, oranges and lemons, figs, dates and sugar. These were all very expensive commodities, especially sugar which was kept locked up and used sparingly. Locally produced honey would have been a much cheaper alternative for sweetening foods and drink. These new items would have found their way onto the banqueting tables as would various wild birds like herons, gulls, quails, blackbirds, and lapwings which would have been trapped in the heath land or caught in the harbour. Wild boar, which was also common locally, goose and venison provided traditional dishes, especially at Christmas. The manorial estates would have had their own hunting rights. Hunting for game has been a sport enjoyed by monarchy and the gentry in this area for centuries.

Christchurch Castle and Constable's House 1783

As fish was such a staple part of the diet, estates often had their own fish pond which was stocked with specially bred tench, carp and pike. The fish pond of the Manor of Somerford estate can still be seen within the Mudeford Wood Conservation Area. A fishery at Knapp which was mentioned in the Domesday record of 1086, belonged to the Priory. The Prior was also presented with the first salmon of the season that was caught in the harbour each year.

The preparation of food and entertaining necessitated the need for large kitchens with fireplaces wide enough to roast a whole animal over a spit. Other dishes were boiled in a large cauldron hanging over the fire. Ovens for baking bread and pies were found only in larger houses and monasteries. The oven was built of brick and clay and was pre-heated by making a fire inside it. When it was sufficiently hot the embers and ash were raked out and the food was placed inside to cook. These methods of cooking remained unaltered for centuries. Many manors had separate buildings for each function: a bake house, a buttery (to serve drinks), a pantry and a dairy as well as the kitchen(s). The Augustinian Priory, in addition to these buildings, also had its own brew house. This building still exists and is situated in a car park near to Christchurch Priory.

People during the Middle Ages did not eat raw food as they thought it was unhealthy. Apparently selling fruit in the street was banned during the time of the plague in case it helped to spread the disease. Fruit and vegetables were cooked or pickled and milk was made into custards, possets, cream soups and cheesecakes.

Medieval Mince Pie *recipe transcribed from Old English by* **Ken Tullett, Archivist of Christchurch Priory:**

Make the pastry by seething (boiling) together lard, water and milk and pouring it onto flour. Mix four times as much minced mutton or beef, to suet and dried fruit to make the filling. Season the mixture with cloves, mace, black pepper, saffron and the zest and juice of an orange. Bake the pie in a hot oven.

The Dissolution of the Monasteries in 1538 had a profound affect on Christchurch. Ownership of the Priory's lands changed hands, ending many of the Medieval ways, including the Feudal System. A new prosperous and influential class, the landed gentry, gradually evolved.

The old manorial estates had large households comprising various relatives and staff and they ate together in the great hall. The new landed gentry had money to lavish on luxuries and they spent time away from their estates, in London, socialising. Their households in London were much smaller and needed less room in which to dine and therefore a dining room was created.

The second half of the 16th century was an exciting age of exploration and increased trade. New foods that explorers brought back from such places as South America included potatoes, tomatoes, walnuts and turkey. On the estates new fruits such as apricots and raspberries were introduced among the existing apple, pear and plum trees.

Banquets were still very visual and made great use of marzipan and especially sugar, which was very popular, for decoration. Fruits were crystallised, and sugar was also spun or made into hard, brittle sheets. In the extreme, this plate sugar was even used to make platters or goblets. The finest tables, now adorned with a linen cloth, were still graced by gold or silver tableware. The central decoration was a large salt cellar. Lesser nobles had wooden bowls and platters and horn or leather drinking vessels. These were gradually replaced by those made of earthenware or pewter.

The period of upheaval and change from the Medieval ways continued well into the 17th century. Until this time dishes, albeit elaborately presented for banquets, had used home or locally produced food which had been cooked by either roasting, boiling or baking. Now there was an interest not only in new flavours but also in new ways of cooking. Royal households used the methods emanating from France which were then copied by those of the prosperous gentry. New drinks of coffee, tea and chocolate proved popular. Coffee shops were very much part of the London scene. Cookery books were being produced and contained recipes such as were used in royal and noble households. These included dishes from overseas.

Developments included new methods of making cakes and biscuits and the introduction of new types of ovens such as the beehive due to its shape in which to cook them. This saw the birth of the sponge cake, gingerbread and biscuits as we know them today. Previously biscuits were really sweetened bread dough. The pudding cloth was invented and this gave rise to a wide range of steamed puddings.

Food was still cooked over the fire. Skillets, a forerunner of our saucepan but with three legs, were introduced. The old kitchen at Grove Farm, Christchurch, which dates from Tudor times has an inglenook fireplace at least 5' wide and 3' deep. Above the fireplace is an iron spit bar for roasting the meat and on each side of the hearth in the brickwork are ledges on which to place the cooking pots and pans. On one side of the recess is the faggot-oven, which burnt 'faggots' of wood, for baking bread.

Hookey's House, Christchurch, which was unfortunately demolished in 1972 dated from Tudor times or even earlier and had a large brick fireplace with a smoke chamber for preserving meat.

Cauldrons continued to be used in the fireplace to boil meat but they were now made sufficiently large to hold the complete meal. The meat was placed in a separate container inside the cauldron; the vegetables in a bag and the pudding in a cloth were placed in the bubbling water. Jugged hare would have been a local dish to have been cooked in this economical way.

The new methods of cooking also prompted the regional variations and specialities in food local examples being apple cake and Dorset Knobs and Whigs and Blue Vinney cheese which would have been produced in the then neighbouring county.

As trade increased and the town prospered during the 18th century many new houses were built. Christchurch, by this time, had a stage coach route up to London and was also on the route between Poole and Lymington. Church Hatch, Millhams Mead and Tyneham House are all extant examples of 'fine town houses' from this time. The Square House, a contemporary but unfortunately no longer in existence, was renowned for its Palladian exterior and fine Adam's style interior design. It was built by John Cook who had already established a brewery at the neighbouring site in the High Street. When he sold The Square

House in 1796 the sale notice described the house as comprising '......cook's kitchen, larder, outer pantry kitchen, housekeeper's store room, butler's glass room, ...'. Glassware was now very much in vogue and damask-covered dinner tables of the gentry would have been graced by wine glasses, tumblers and special dishes for ice-cream, syllabubs and other desserts. By the end of the 17th century knives and forks were in general use (spoons had been in use for some time) and the preferred metal for cutlery was silver. Ordinary folk used pewter and earthenware for their cutlery and crockery.

Gustavus Brander, who was responsible for demolishing the old manor house at Somerford and erecting the grand Somerford Grange in its place, had already built Priory House complete with an ice house within its 30 acres of land. Ice cream was introduced into London during the late 1600s and its popularity spread. Many local manor houses or country seats such as Hurn Court, Hurn; the Manor of Funckton (the farm house of Merritown Farm being only part of the original manor house) and Nea House, Highcliffe had ice houses built on their land. Hinton Wood Avenue was known as Ice House Hill and the ice house was still marked on early 20th century Ordnance Survey maps. Ice houses were dug deep into the ground and insulated with straw so that winter ice could be kept all year round.

The cooks in these new houses would have been kept busy with the entertaining that was expected of the family as well as cooking the family's meals. Syllabub, which was originally a Christmas drink made from milk and wine or ale, became popular as a dessert. At this time pasta, curry and rice and ketchup from China were introduced into our cuisine. Other trends included the increased use of sugar in cooking, as opposed to its use in decoration, and the move away from the traditional spices, flavourings and coloured foods. Butter and alcohol were lavishly used in cooking but the dishes themselves became simplified; sauces, for example having only one flavouring. It was fashionable to employ a French cook, though not to cook French food! The reason for this was mainly patriotism. Although French chefs were considered the best, we were at war with France for much of this period.

By the middle of the 18th century the national dish was said to be roast beef followed by plum pudding as the dessert. Roasting was now the favoured method of cooking meat and new ovens had been invented in which meat could be roasted. It was also possible to bake a batter pudding in the same oven. Only the rich would have been able to afford one of these ovens. People who did not have their own oven and wished to bake a pie would send it to the local bakery, uncooked, with their initials marked in the crust.

The kitchen range was introduced into houses towards the end of the century. As wood was in short supply in Christchurch peat turves were generally used for fuel. 'Rights of turbary' were allowed for the commoners to cut peat from the common land (Town Common). People could now stew meat or fruit and make jam. Making sauces was much easier too.

As tea became the nation's favourite drink (much of it smuggled) it was common to see a cast iron kettle hanging over the fire in the fireplace beside the cauldron.

It was now accepted that it was safe to eat raw fruit and vegetables and many large houses had hot houses in their grounds where they could grow more exotic kinds. One wonders if the uncooked fruit and vegetables were mainly for show as the diet of all but the labouring classes was very unhealthy. Refined bread was very popular as was sweet food. Smoking and too much alcohol (this was the great age of smuggling in Christchurch), excessive amounts of sugar and fatty foods, insufficient fibre and a lack of exercise gave rise to many health problems: cirrhosis of the liver, diabetes, gout and heart problems.

The reaction was to eat a healthier diet and exercise more. New houses being built, Hengistbury House and Ashtree House in Purewell and Bure Homage at Mudeford, for example, had green and hot houses built in which to grow their own produce. They also had kitchen gardens, orchards and pasture or arable land. The new healthy trend promoted the use of health spas and sea-swimming. Avon Beach, owing to its 'pure water and fine level beach' became popular for swimming especially after George III's visit to Sandhills, owned by Sir George Rose, at the beginning of the 19th century and the numerous bathing machines in the bay became a familiar sight.

Mudeford, therefore, was considered to be a desirable place to visit and many new properties were built during this period of the late 18th and early 19th centuries including High Cliff, its successor Highcliffe Castle and Bure Homage both built by Lord Stuart de Rothesay, Gundimore, Mudeford House and Avonmouth House. Many famous and distinguished people visited the area and socialised with the local gentry. Sir Walter Scott stayed at Gundimore and Avenue Cottage was used by Lt. Col. Monkton to put up guests who had been invited to his shooting parties. Sir Arthur Conan Doyle was one such guest. Due to the popularity of the area, many people took in summer visitors and gentry such as Lord Stuart de Rothesay and the Camerons at Nea House let their houses for the season while they were either in London or travelling abroad.

Christchurch Harbour showing Avonmouth House 1861

Increased literacy meant that book production was prolific and cookery books proved very popular. Many of these books were written by women and they often included medical recipes and hints on household chores and management. Therefore any servant who could read could better themselves and theoretically become a reasonable cook.

Until the mid 19th century the food that was eaten by most people was still whatever could be obtained locally - from the markets, local shops or what they could supply for themselves. Farms provided much of the meat consumed. Bread was still an important part of the diet especially for the lower classes when many of whom lost valuable land or small holdings due to the Inclosure of Land Acts.

With the advent of the railways came an improved variety of foods available. Due to the speed and ease of journeys perishable food was fresher too. It was not until a little later that canned foods were available and 1880 saw the beginning of refrigeration and the transportation of bulk meat.

Modifications were made to ovens producing a greater resemblance to today's ovens, though cooking over a fire in the fireplace still continued into the 20th century. The early 20th century saw the introduction of gas cookers and grills which were soon to be rivalled by electricity.

The Victorian kitchen had an inordinate number of specific pots, pans, dishes, glasses and tools that were used. There were pans for milk, for omelettes, for sautéing and frying as well as different sized saucepans; there were fish kettles, jelly moulds and patty pans. Specialised tools included pastry and biscuit cutters, choppers, peelers, graters and mincers. Towards the end of this period these devices began to be mechanised, leading us into the labour-saving ways of the 20th century.

A noticeable difference in our present attitude to food compared to that of the Victorians was that they spent an enormous amount of time planning, preparing for and eating meals. Breakfast was substantial and comprised a choice of hot dishes such as bacon, sausage, eggs, kidneys, chops, steaks and kippers; a selection of cold or potted meats and fish, hot or cold pies as well as toast and butter with home-made jam or marmalade. Dinner was served later in the evening than in previous centuries because the head of the household in general had to travel to town for his work and therefore spent a large proportion of the day away from home. Dinner parties were common and the status of the host was reflected in the amount and variety of food served. A modest dinner party could have as many as a dozen different courses. Even family meals were extensive by our standards and choices were given. Mrs Beeton suggested, in her cookery book, a suitable family dinner for a Monday evening to be: baked soles to start; cold veal and bacon with salad or mutton cutlets and tomato sauce as the main dish followed by boiled currant pudding. Sorbets were often served between courses, especially at dinner parties, to clean the palate. Much thought was given to decorating the table at meal times and it was a must to include napkins elegantly folded and a bowl or vase of flowers, even at breakfast time! It must be remembered, though, that Victorian families were large and that households had servants to assist the cook and the butler.

In 1907, the Emperor of Germany spent some weeks at Highcliffe Castle and on the advice of Edward VII, Mrs Rosa Lewis was engaged to cook for the Kaiser during his stay. Rosa moved into Highcliffe from London and began arranging the catering for the Emperor and his large entourage. Mrs Violet Stuart Wortley in her memoirs reminisces 'The first lunch was a rather trying one. Unfortunately quails were on the menu, and as I sat next to His Majesty I became aware that this item was an unfortunate selection. With only his one hand available, the knife-and-fork instrument H.M. used sent the bird skidding round his plate, and the pursuit of the bird became hectic.'

Highcliffe Castle 1907

Another problem soon presented itself. The small village shops, unprepared for the large demands made of them, soon ran out of stock and so Rosa had to go to London everyday, travelling in state by the special train, to buy her groceries at Jackson's of Piccadilly and the remaining produce from Covent Garden.

The Second World War altered the lifestyle of people drastically. From the beginning of 1940 many foods began to be rationed and diets changed accordingly. Foods that were not rationed included potatoes, flour, seasonal fruits and vegetables. People were encouraged to grow their own - to 'Dig for Victory'. Some town dwellers also kept chickens for their eggs. Wartime recipes used dried milk and egg as ingredients. Meat, sugar, butter, margarine, cooking fat, treacle and sweets were all rationed during the war. Imported fruits such as oranges and bananas were impossible to obtain. Despite the restrictions, the food available produced a healthy diet. Vegetables augmented the meagre rations (by our standards) of meat, fish and eggs. People valued food and did not waste it. Throughout the war the Ministry of Food published 'Food Facts' to help people devise the best methods of using scarce and rationed foods. They also encouraged people to try different combinations of tastes such as watercress butter spread on toast. Watercress, which would have occurred naturally in the local rivers and had been commercially produced since the late 19th century, has a high iron content. The Christchurch Times contained many such food facts and recipes to promote healthy eating.

Welsh Rarebit - *wartime style from* **Linda Arnold, Red House Museum**

For 1 helping toast 2 slices of bread and spread with 1 teaspoon of margarine. Add a thin coating of chutney (1 teaspoon) and 1 tablespoon of grated cheese per slice of toast. Replace under the grill until it is golden brown and serve with a raw vegetable salad.

Saving fuel during the war years was important and so steaming, where many dishes could be cooked together over one pan of water, was popular as was the use of the hay-box. Stews were placed in the conventional oven to begin their cooking and then transferred to the hay-box to complete the cooking process. Catering for larger groups of people also helped to save on fuel. Schools provided dinners for children, factories had canteens for their workers and the large number of restaurants produced inexpensive meals. An upper limit was imposed on them for the amount of money they could charge for each meal.

The other major factor which has shaped the food industry over the last century is the enormous changes in technology. The general availability of electricity has enabled processors and other labour saving kitchen devices to become highly mechanised and efficient. Virtually all households now have a refrigerator, so food is kept fresher for longer, and most people have a freezer. This has led to a change in food shopping patterns. We now tend to buy food in bulk and not as we require it. We no longer have to buy foods when they are in season. The canning and freezing industries have provided us with foods from any part of the world whenever we require them.

Another advance that has been made is the introduction of cooking food by microwave- a totally new concept. Once again there has been an emphasis on promoting a healthy diet to correct our lifestyle our existence on junk food and take-aways, snacking rather than eating a proper meal because we are too busy and a lack of exercise.

Delicious Home-made 5 Minute Muesli *from* **The Bay Tree**, *Christchurch.*

100g (4 oz) organic jumbo oats
A handful jumbo seedless raisins
Fruit Juice (orange, pineapple, apple, grapefruit)
6-8 stewed apricots, diced
5 tablespoon live Biogarde yoghurt
2 tablespoon nuts (pecans, hazelnuts, walnuts)

Place the jumbo oats and raisins in a bowl and add sufficient fruit juice to cover them. Leave the bowl overnight in the fridge.

Add the apricots (or other fruit of your choice) and the yoghurt and top with the nuts to produce a delicious and nutritious breakfast for two people.

The news from the late 20th century is full of food scares from listeria and mad cow disease to the concern about genetically modified foods and the plight of British farmers. As we settle down to watch one of the many cookery programmes on television for entertainment, with our reheated microwaveable ready-cooked meal we may well wonder what the cuisine of the 21st century will have to offer.

Soups, Snacks and Starters

Snacking is a late 20th century trend. It implies that because we are so busy we do not have time to sit down and eat a proper meal. However snacks do not have to be unhealthy as our recipes show.

In the past the first course of a meal was much more expansive and extravagant than today's 'starter' and consisted of a number of diverse dishes giving ample choice for each person. The modern equivalent would be a buffet. For example, the central dishes for the first course of a dinner (of five courses) for King George II were a green pottage of lambs heads, a pottage of partridges and a plate of mixed meats, Spanish style. Other dishes, placed on the table in a symmetrical pattern, comprised a haunch of venison, chine of mutton and veal, boiled goose and savoys, a chine of bacon and turkey, a green and a white salad, Dutch butter and a pickled herring salad.

The second course usually comprised lighter meats, game and some sweet foods. This particular second course contained a mixture of tarts, custards and cheesecakes as well as dishes containing a central jelly with shrimps, artichokes, potatoes, mushrooms, asparagus and eggs with gravy arranged around them. Other dishes on the sideboard to compliment the meal included tripe cooked by a French method, broiled herrings, pheasants, partridges and quails, cocks, plovers and snipes, roast teal, a collar of brawn, fried cream, a dish of minced pies and a venison pasty.

Salmon Fishing at Mudeford c.1900

Warm Salad of Seared Scallops
and Cherry Tomatoes
with Sesame and Honey Dressing

Eddie Blanchard
The Ship in Distress, Stanpit

Serves 4

8 large shelled scallops with coral/roe
16 cherry tomatoes
100g (3½ oz) corn salad (or mixed salad leaves)
A few basil leaves
Olive oil

Dressing

4 tablespoons extra virgin olive oil
2 teaspoons clear honey
1 tablespoon balsamic vinegar
2 teaspoons sesame seeds, toasted
Salt and freshly ground pepper

Slice the scallops into three discs each, one with the coral still attached. Wash the corn salad and picked basil leaves.

Using a small bowl, mix all the dressing ingredients together.

Pre-heat a wok to smoking hot. Put in a little olive oil and drop in the scallops. Flash fry to lightly caramelise then remove the scallops with a slotted spoon.

Briefly fry the cherry tomatoes in the same oil. Remove from the heat. Add the corn salad, basil, scallops and dressing. Toss quickly to coat.

To serve, arrange on four plates.

Note: If you don't have a wok a heavy frying pan may be used.

Thai Spiced Crab Tortellini

James Penn, Head Chef
Waterford Lodge Hotel

Serves 8 for a starter or 4 for a light meal

Pasta Dough

      450g (1 lb) strong white flour
      1 teaspoon salt
      75ml (2½ fl oz) olive oil
      225ml (7½ fl oz) water

      or use 450g (1 lb) fresh pasta

Tortellini filling

      1 teaspoon olive oil
      1 teaspoon garlic, peeled and crushed
      2 teaspoons shallots, chopped
      4 teaspoons mixed peppers, finely diced
      1 small red chilli, halved, seeded, finely diced
      60g (2 oz) beansprouts, roughly chopped
      2 spring onions, chopped
      60g (2 oz) fresh coriander leaves, roughly chopped
      225g (8 oz) white crab meat
      1 or 2 teaspoons Thai red curry paste (to taste)
      1 teaspoon tomato purée

Sauce

      450ml (15 fl oz) good shellfish or fish stock
      2 teaspoons peeled root ginger, grated
      3 teaspoons tomato purée

To make the pasta dough: Place all the ingredients into a food processor, process until large lumps form. Knead on a lightly floured surface for two to three minutes to smooth.

Wrap in cling film and chill for one hour.

To make the filling: Heat olive oil, add garlic, shallots, peppers and chilli, sweat for 2-3 minutes until softened. Add beansprouts and spring onion, cook a further 1-2 minutes. Add coriander, crab meat, curry paste and tomato purée. Mix well on a low heat for 1 minute. Season to taste with salt and pepper and set aside.

Pass the pasta dough through a pasta machine to the one before thinnest setting. Using a 9 cm (3½ in) plain round cutter, cut out as many circles as you can. Brush the edge of each circle with beaten egg, place a heaped teaspoon of the crab mixture in the centre and fold over to form a semicircle eliminating as much air as possible. Press the edges together to seal. With the straight edge towards you, bring the ends together, creating a lip around the crescent, and press the ends together with a little beaten egg to join them. Keep in a cool place in a single layer between sheets of non-stick baking parchment while preparing the sauce.

Place the shellfish stock, ginger and tomato purée in a wide shallow pan. Bubble to reduce to coating consistency. Draw aside and keep warm.

Bring a large pan of well-salted water to the boil. Add a few drops of oil to prevent sticking. Add the tortellini and cook for approximately 5 minutes, until "al dente". Drain well.

To serve, spoon the sauce on to the base of the serving plates then place the tortellini on the sauce.

Cheese Apple Flowers

Lyn Taylor

Serves 4

> 1 x 200g (7 oz) Philadelphia cheese
> ½ teaspoon each of chopped fresh parsley, mint, chives
> 2 bright red apples, washed and dried
> Juice of 1 lemon
> Lettuce leaves, washed and dried
> 4 sprigs of mint, to garnish
> Salt and freshly ground pepper

Place the cheese, herbs and seasoning in a bowl, beat well to mix together, chill.

Pour the lemon juice into a wide necked, screw-top jar. Quarter the apples and carefully remove the cores. Slice each quarter into three. Place the slices into the jar, screw on the lid and gently turn the jar round and round to ensure every part of the apples are coated to prevent discoloration.

Form four rounds (ball shaped) with the cheese. Place a lettuce leaf on each serving plate and place a round of cheese on each. Drain the apples and gently, but firmly, push a pointed end of each slice of the apples into the cheese to form petals (rather like water lilies). Place a sprig of mint in the centre. Chill.

Serve with brown bread and butter.

Note: These can be made 24 hours before eating.

Butter and Garlic King Prawns

Steve Sun-Sangman
Lychee Chinese Restaurant

Serves 2

12 unshelled king prawns
½ teaspoon sesame oil
Salt and freshly ground pepper
1 tablespoon cornflour
Oil for deep frying
2 tablespoons butter
2 teaspoons crushed garlic or flakes
1 spring onion, finely chopped
½ teaspoon five spice powder
1 tablespoon Shaoxing cooking wine or dry sherry
2 iceberg lettuce leaves, finely chopped
1 small carrot, peeled and finely chopped.

Wash the prawns, remove the centre section of shell of each prawn, keeping the heads and tails on, and remove the centre vein. Season the prawns with salt and pepper and flavour with sesame oil. Toss in cornflour to coat and leave for 20 minutes. Using a deep fat fryer heat the oil until hot and fry the prawns until cooked, for approximately 1 - 2 minutes. Remove.

Using a frying or sauté pan gently heat the butter to melt. Stir in the garlic and spring onions. Add the prawns, toss to coat. Season with salt, pepper and five spice powder. Add the wine.

To serve, garnish two plates with the lettuce and carrot and arrange the prawns with heads facing the same way.

Crab Parfait with Spiced Cucumber Relish

Ian Morton, Head Chef
The Avonmouth Hotel

Serves 6

<u>Crab Parfait</u>

450g (1 lb) brown crab meat
2 drops of Tabasco sauce
2 drops of Worcestershire sauce
4 sheets gelatine, soaked for 5 minutes in cold water to soften
3 tablespoons water
300ml (10 fl oz) whipping or double cream
Salt and freshly ground pepper

<u>Spiced Cucumber Relish</u>

1 large cucumber
60g (2 oz) caster sugar
60ml (2 fl oz) white wine vinegar
300ml (10 fl oz) water
A good pinch of ground mixed spice
1 red pepper, halved, seeded and diced

Have ready 6 individual ramekin dishes.

To make the crab parfait: Place the crab meat, Tabasco and Worcestershire sauces into a blender or food processor and work to a purée, season with salt and pepper.

Using a small pan heat the water. Squeeze the gelatine lightly from its soaking liquid and place it in the hot water to melt. Stir into the crab mixture.

Using a large bowl whisk the cream to leave a thick trail. Fold into the crab mixture. Fill the ramekins and refrigerate to set.

To make the cucumber relish: Peel the cucumber and dice the skin. Halve the cucumber lengthways, remove the seeds and coarsely grate or finely slice the flesh. Place the sugar, vinegar, water and mixed spice into a pan, bring to the boil. Remove from the heat and cool. Mix together the cucumber, diced cucumber skin, diced pepper and the spiced vinegar mixture. Season and chill.

To serve, place a ramekin on each individual serving plate and some cucumber relish on the plate next to it. Cucumbers vary in water content so leave excess spiced dressing behind as necessary. Serve with toast or brown bread and butter.

Spicy Prawn Salad

Ann Bread

Serves 4

> 350g (12 oz) cooked peeled prawns
> 280g (10 oz) celery, chopped
> 1 medium pineapple, peeled and chopped
> Half iceberg lettuce, washed, dried and shredded

Curry Dressing

> 150ml (5 fl oz) mayonnaise
> 1 tablespoon mild curry paste
> 3 tablespoons mango chutney
> 2 tablespoons chopped fresh coriander leaves
> Salt and pepper

Mix together the prawns, celery and pineapple. In another bowl flavour the mayonnaise with the curry paste and mango chutney. Season well with salt and pepper. Gently stir the prawn mixture into the curry dressing with the coriander.

To serve, pile the lettuce leaves on to four plates and top with the prawn mixture and serve with warm naan bread.

Spinach and Feta Cheese Tartlets

Mary Reader
Reader Communications

This is a versatile dish to prepare for a lacto-vegetarian or to serve for a buffet party or as a starter.

Serves 4

1 sheet of ready rolled puff pastry
30g (1 oz) butter
1 small onion, chopped
225g (8 oz) baby spinach leaves
115g (4 oz) cream cheese
60g (2 oz) feta cheese
1 large egg
Salt and freshly ground pepper

Pre-heat the oven to 220°C/425°F/Gas 7.

Divide the pastry and roll out into four circles. Use each circle to line a small flan tin 8½ cm (3½ in). Melt the butter and gently fry the onions for 5 minutes until softened. Add the spinach and cook until wilted for 2 minutes. Remove from the heat.

Stir in the cream cheese, feta cheese and egg. Season carefully (feta cheese is naturally salty).

Pour the mixture into the pastry tartlets. Place them on a baking sheet and bake in the oven for 10 - 15 minutes.

Serve with a side salad of baby spinach leaves, feta cheese and black olives.

Opposite: *Spinach and Feta Cheese Tartlets*
Next page: *Thai Spiced Crab Tortellini (see p.18)*

Ciabatta Special

The Coffee Pot
Bargates, Christchurch

Serves 1

1½ teaspoons green pesto
1½ teaspoons mayonnaise
1 ciabatta roll
Friseé lettuce
75g (2½ oz) cooked chicken, sliced
2 rashers crisply grilled bacon
2 whole mushrooms grilled, then sliced
Sliced cucumber
Sliced tomato
Freshly ground black pepper

In a bowl, thoroughly mix the pesto and mayonnaise.

Cut the ciabatta roll in half lengthways and spread both cut surfaces evenly with the pesto mix.

Layer the bottom half with the friseé lettuce followed with the sliced chicken, bacon rashers, sliced mushrooms, cucumber and tomato. Season with freshly ground black pepper.

Sandwich together with the other half of the roll and eat.

Previous page: *Fishing in Christchurch Harbour*
Opposite: *Warm Goats Cheese and Tomato Tart (see p.32)*

Wild Mushroom and Game Terrine

Marcel Duval
Le Petit St. Tropez, Christchurch

Serves 6

50g (1¾ oz) Parma ham, thinly sliced
12 pigeon breasts
200g (7 oz) rabbit fillet
2 quails, boned completely
200g (7 oz) venison saddle, trimmed
600ml (1 pint) game consommé
2 sheets gelatine, soaked for 5 minutes in cold water
250g (9 oz) fresh wild mushrooms as available, *e.g. cèpes, chanterelles, girolle, pied bleu*
50g (1¾ oz) dried shiitake mushrooms, soaked overnight
A little olive oil and butter
½ tablespoon chopped fresh chives
½ tablespoon chopped fresh chervil
Salt and freshly ground black pepper

Line a 1 litre (1¾ pint) capacity terrine mould with cling film and then the Parma ham.

Cut all game into 1 cm (½ in) strips and poach in a little of the consommé, keeping the venison and pigeon slightly pink.

Warm the remaining consommé, squeeze out the gelatine and add to the consommé. Allow it to melt then leave to cool. Wash, trim and clean all the mushrooms thoroughly, slice them and sauté in a little hot olive oil and butter. Drain, season and add the chopped herbs, cool.

Assemble the terrine by layering the mushroom and game. Finally add the cool consommé and gelatine to come level with the top layer. Refrigerate to set. When set, lay 2 layers of foil or cling film on top and press under 750g – 1 kg (1½ - 2 lb) weight for 8 hours in a refrigerator.

To serve, turn out and slice. Lay on a salad of rocket and spider endive (or frisée) with warm brioche and fruity based chutney.

Note: Canned game consommé is readily available.

Smoked Haddock Paté

Sue Randle
Christchurch Council

Serves 6

450g (1 lb) smoked haddock, cooked
3 tablespoons lemon juice
1 sachet gelatine
300ml (10 fl oz) whipping cream
2 eggs, hard boiled then finely chopped
2 tablespoons chopped fresh parsley
Salt and freshly ground black pepper
Lemon wedges and watercress to garnish

Have ready an 850ml (1½ pint) capacity terrine or ring mould.

Remove the skin and bones from the fish, place the flesh into a blender and process to a purée and transfer into a bowl. Put the lemon juice into a small cup or small bowl, sprinkle on the gelatine and leave until spongy. Stand the cup in a pan of barely simmering water until the gelatine has melted or melt the gelatine in a microwave oven. Remove from the water and leave to cool.

Whisk the cream until it leaves a trail, but would still just run if the bowl is tilted. Gently mix the gelatine into the fish with the eggs and parsley. Fold in the cream and season to taste. Turn the mixture into the mould and refrigerate for four hours to set.

To serve, turn the paté out on to a plate and garnish with the lemon wedges and watercress.

Note: If using a ring mould you could turn out then fill the centre with shelled prawns and garnish with whole prawns.

Warm Goat's Cheese and Tomato Tart
with Mixed Salad Leaves in a Pesto Dressing

David Ryan, Chef Patron
The Bistro on the Beach

Serves 4

225g (8 oz) puff pastry
1 egg yolk plus 1 tablespoon water beaten together

Filling

60g (2 oz) butter
115g (4 oz) onion, chopped
1 clove garlic, peeled and chopped
900g (2 lb) beef tomatoes, seeded and chopped
100ml (3½ fl oz) dry white wine
300ml (10 fl oz) pure tomato juice
1 teaspoon tomato purée
Freshly milled black pepper and salt
Fresh basil leaves
1 small crotin (goats cheese), sliced

Pesto dressing

60g (2 oz) pine kernels
60g (2 oz) Parmesan cheese, grated
125ml (4 fl oz) extra virgin olive oil
1 bunch of fresh basil leaves

Garnish

Mixed salad leaves (frisée, corn salad and rocket)

Lightly butter a baking tray.

To prepare the pastry: Roll out the puff pastry thinly to 2.5 mm thickness. Cut into 2 equal pieces, lay one on top of the other and brush over the surface with the yolk and water. Chill for 15 minutes then cut out 4 x 10 cm (4 in) circles. Now cut out the centres of the top layer only using a 5 cm (2 in) lightly oiled round cutter. Lay the 4 pastry circles on to the baking tray, well apart to allow for expansion, chill.

32

To make the filling: Heat the butter in a pan, add the onion and garlic. Cook on low heat for a few minutes until soft, but not coloured. Add the tomatoes and wine, increase the heat and bubble, stirring frequently, until the mixture has reduced by half. Now add the tomato juice and purée and cook on very low heat for 1 hour. Season and set aside to cool.

Pre-heat the oven to 200-220°C/400°F-425°F/Gas 6-7. On top of each tart base place, a teaspoon of the filling and basil leaves. Top with a slice of the goats cheese. Bake for 5 - 7 minutes or until golden brown.

To prepare the pesto dressing: Place all ingredients into a food processor and process all the ingredients to a smooth paste.

To serve, place each tart in the centre of a plate and surround with a mixture of salad leaves previously tossed in the pesto dressing.

Thai Prawns in Coconut

Mary Reader
Reader Communications

Serves 4

1 tablespoon dried lemon grass
1 teaspoon dried hot chillies
1 teaspoon dried coriander
1 teaspoon garlic
2 kaffir lime leaves
2 shallots, finely chopped
1 tablespoon sugar
200ml (7 fl oz) coconut cream
450g (1 lb) raw prawns, peeled

In a medium bowl combine the lemon grass, chilli, coriander, garlic, kaffir lime leaves, shallots and sugar. Mix together with the coconut cream. Pour into a wok and heat gently for 10 minutes.

Add the prawns and cook for 3 minutes or until the prawns are cooked, stirring frequently to make sure the prawns are coated with the sauce.

Remove the kaffir lime leaves. Serve at once with rice.

Lemon Chicken Soup

Susan Eckstein

Serves 4

> 30g (1 oz) butter
> 1 small onion, peeled and thinly sliced
> 30g (1 oz) flour
> 850ml (1½ pints) good strong chicken stock
> Salt and freshly ground pepper
> Finely pared rind of half a lemon
> 2 tablespoons lemon juice
> 90ml (3 fl oz) whipping cream or creme fraîche
> 1 teaspoon chopped fresh parsley

In a medium saucepan melt the butter, add the onion. Cover and cook on a very low heat until soft, but not coloured, for about 10 minutes.

Stir in the flour and cook on a low heat for 1 minute. Pour in the stock and stir until boiling. Add the lemon rind and ¾ of the lemon juice. Season lightly, cover and simmer for 15 minutes.

Strain and return to the rinsed pan and add the cream. Re-season adding the remaining lemon juice to taste.

To serve, re-heat and pour into warm soup bowls and sprinkle with the parsley.

Variations: Add a few cooked shelled prawns or mussels before re-heating and sprinkle with chervil leaves. A pinch of saffron soaked in 2 tablespoons of hot water and added to the stock is delicious with shellfish. This makes an ideal soup for a special occasion.

Broccoli and Garlic Soup

Susan Eckstein

Serves 4

> 1 tablespoon oil
> 2 large garlic cloves, peeled and halved
> 850ml (1½ pints) chicken or vegetable stock
> 450g (1 lb) broccoli
> Salt and freshly ground black pepper

In a small pan heat the oil. Add the garlic and gently fry until golden. Remove the pan from the hob, lift out the garlic and keep it to one side.

In a medium saucepan bring the stock to the boil. Meanwhile, cut 30g (1 oz) of tiny flowerettes from the broccoli and reserve them for garnish. Trim the remaining heads from the stalks and cut stalks roughly into 1 cm (½ in) pieces.

Add the heads and cut stalks to the hot stock. Season lightly with salt and pepper and add garlic. Cover and simmer for 20 minutes.

To prepare the garnish: While the soup is cooking, bring a small pan of lightly salted water to the boil, add the reserved flowerettes and cook, uncovered for 2 minutes. Drain and run under cold water to stop them overcooking. Drain well.

Remove the soup from the hob, pour into a liquidiser and blend until smooth. Rinse out the pan and pour soup back into it.

To serve, re-heat the soup, taste and re-season as necessary. Add the garnish and pour into warm soup bowls.

Salada Horiatiki
(Village-style Greek Salad)

Chris Panaretou
Christopher Mark Hairdessing, Christchurch

Serves 6

1 Cos lettuce, chopped
½ cucumber, chopped
1 stick celery, finely chopped
115g (4 oz) white cabbage, finely chopped
115g (4 oz) tomatoes, chopped
115g (4 oz) onions, chopped with a few rings for garnish
115g (4 oz) black olives, unpitted
115g (4 oz) feta cheese, cubed
2 tablespoons white wine vinegar
4 tablespoons extra virgin olive oil
Salt and freshly ground black pepper

In a small bowl mix together the vinegar and oil and season with salt and pepper. Place the remaining ingredients in a serving bowl keeping a few olives, pieces of cheese and the onion rings on one side for the garnish. Pour the dressing over the salad and garnish with the onion, cheese and olives.

The perfect accompaniment to most meat and fish dishes or just on its own.

Houmous
(Chick Pea Dip)

Chris Panaretou
Christopher Mark Hairdessing, Christchurch

Serves 6

225g (8 oz) cracked chick peas
½ teaspoon bicarbonate of soda
3 cloves of garlic, crushed
Juice of 1½ lemons
2 tablespoons tahini paste
4 tablespoons olive oil
Salt and ground white pepper

Garnish

Ground paprika
Olive oil
1 tablespoon finely chopped parsley

Place the chick peas into a saucepan, add the bicarbonate of soda and cover with water. Leave to soak overnight.

Drain the peas and add cold water to cover then bring to the boil. Cover with a lid and simmer for 1½ hours or until tender. Drain the peas, reserving one cupful of the liquid, and leave to cool.

Put the peas, garlic, lemon juice, tahini paste and half the reserved liquid into a blender and blend until smooth. Add the remaining liquid, olive oil, salt and pepper. Mix well until thoroughly combined. Pour into a serving dish and garnish with the parsley, some paprika and a little olive oil drizzled over the top.

Serve with warmed pitta bread.

Red Mullet Broth

Gary Webster
Manor Arms, Burton

Serves 4

4 fillets red mullet
4 slices Parma ham – each cut into 4 strips
2 plum tomatoes, skinned, seeded and diced
60g (2 oz) butter, cut into cubes and chilled
A few fresh tarragon leaves
Sea salt and freshly ground black pepper

Red Mullet Stock

30g (1 oz) butter
1 onion, peeled and roughly diced
1 carrot, peeled and roughly diced
1 leek washed and roughly diced
3 celery sticks, roughly diced
1 fennel bulb, roughly diced
1 clove of garlic, peeled and crushed
½ bunch of fresh tarragon, approx. 8g (¼ oz)
A pinch of saffron
1 star anise
4 tomatoes, quartered
350g (12 oz) red mullet bones, including head
300ml (10 fl oz) dry white wine
1 litre (1¾ pints) fish stock.

The Soup

1-2 tablespoons olive oil
1 carrot, peeled and diced
2 celery sticks, diced
1 small fennel bulb, diced
Red mullet stock

To make the red mullet stock: In a large saucepan heat the butter, add the vegetables, tarragon, saffron and star anise. Cook on low heat until they begin to soften. Add the tomato and garlic and continue to cook for a few minutes to soften. Add the red mullet bones and cook for 3 minutes on medium heat, add the wine, increase the heat and allow the wine to bubble and reduce by three-quarters. Pour in the fish stock and bring to a gentle simmer. Simmer for 20 - 30 minutes then strain through a fine sieve and discard the fish and vegetables.

To make the soup: In a medium pan heat enough olive oil to barely coat the base, add the vegetables and cook without colouring for 6 minutes.

Pour on the strained red mullet stock and simmer for 10 minutes.

To cook the fish and Parma ham: While the soup is cooking, preheat the grill and lightly butter a baking tray. Place the red mullet fillets on the tray, season with salt and pepper and grill for 3 - 4 minutes and grill the Parma ham until crispy.

To finish the broth and serve: Whisk the butter into the soup a little at a time then stir in the tomatoes, season and add the tarragon.

Pour the broth into warm pasta plates or large, wide, deep soup plates. Place a fillet in each then the ham on each fillet.

For a little extra touch, garnish with deep fried crisp basil or tarragon leaves. Ensure they are dry before frying in hot oil.

Zuppa di Funghi di Bosco
(Wild Mushroom Soup)

Antonio Maggio Carluccio
Pinocchios, Christchurch

Serves 4

450g (1 lb) fresh ceps
[or 450g (1 lb) field mushrooms and 30g (1 oz) fresh ceps]
1 medium onion, finely chopped
4 tablespoons olive oil
1 litre (1¾ pint) beef stock
4 tablespoons double cream
Salt and freshly ground black pepper

If using fresh ceps, clean them and cut into pieces. Cook the chopped onion in the olive oil for 3 - 4 minutes, then add the ceps and sauté them for 6 - 7 minutes.

Add the stock, bring to the boil, then reduce the heat and simmer for 20 minutes. Remove the pan from the heat and leave to cool then blend the contents in a food processor. Return the soup to the pan, add the cream, season with salt and pepper and heat through slowly. Do not boil.

Serve hot, sprinkled with croutons if wished.

Cappelletti in Brodo di Pollo
(Cappelletti in Chicken Broth)

Serves 4

1 litre (1¾ pint) chicken stock
100g (3½ oz) dried capelletti or 200g (7 oz) fresh capelletti
30g (1 oz) freshly grated Parmesan cheese

Bring the stock to the boil add the cappelletti. Bring back to the boil, then reduce the heat and simmer for 10 - 15 minutes until the pasta is cooked.

Serve sprinkled with the Parmesan cheese.

Glazed Salmon Croissant

Kevin Brown, Head Chef
The Lord Bute, Highcliffe

Serves 1

175-200g (6-7 oz) salmon fillet
Salt and freshly ground pepper
A few drops of lemon juice
1 croissant
1 tomato, skinned, seeded and chopped
A few salad leaves

Béarnaise Sauce

1 tablespoon white wine
2 tablespoons white wine vinegar
1 sprig of fresh tarragon, chopped
4 peppercorns
1 egg yolk
125ml (4 fl oz) clarified butter, lukewarm and liquid

Pre-heat the grill to highest setting and pre-heat the oven to 160°C/315°F/Gas 2 - 3.

To prepare the salmon: Season the salmon with a little salt, pepper and lemon juice. Grill the salmon to lightly colour then remove to the oven to cook through, whilst preparing the béarnaise sauce.

To prepare the béarnaise sauce: In a small pan place the wine, wine vinegar, tarragon and peppercorns and heat to reduce by two thirds, then strain into a bowl. Place the bowl over a saucepan of hot water and whisk the egg yolk in. Slowly add the clarified butter whisking continuously until you have a thick, creamy consistency.

To serve, cut the croissant in half lengthways and lightly grill. Place the two halves on to a serving plate, cut sides uppermost and flake the salmon on top. Put tomato on to the salmon and coat with the béarnaise sauce. Glaze under a hot grill.

Serve the glazed salmon croissant with a little fresh salad and some minted new potatoes.

Half Moon Chicken Croquettes

The Boathouse
Quomps, Christchurch

Makes about 12

<u>Pastry</u>

½ cup margarine
½ cup milk
½ plain flour
Salt and pepper

<u>Filling</u>

1 white onion, grated
1 clove of garlic, chopped
1 cup mixed peppers, diced
1 small bunch flat leaf parsley
1 small bunch coriander
60g (2 oz) fresh ginger, finely diced
½ red chilli
1 chicken breast, diced
400g (14 oz) tin of chopped plum tomatoes
1 tablespoon tomato purée
1 tablespoon olive oil

Breadcrumbs, beaten egg and a little flour for coating

To make the pastry: Put all the pastry ingredients in a saucepan and cook over a medium heat, stirring until the mixture comes away from the sides of the pan. Transfer the mixture to a plate and allow to cool completely.

To make the filling: Fry the onion, garlic, peppers and spices in olive oil. Add the chicken and cook for 5 minutes, stirring. Add the tomatoes and tomato purée and cook over a medium heat for 10 minutes until the juices have reduced and the filling is thick and not runny. Set aside to cool completely.

To prepare the croquettes: Take the pastry and roll out thinly onto a floured surface. Cut out 6 cm (2.5 inch) circles and place a little of the chicken mixture in the centre of each circle. Fold into half moon shapes and seal the edges using a fork.

Coat in flour, egg and breadcrumbs and deep fry in hot oil for about 3 minutes until golden brown.

Green Lentil, Bacon & Chirizo Soup

The Boathouse
Quomps, Christchurch

Serves 6

2 cloves of garlic
2 white onions, grated
450g (1 lb) dry green lentils
Juice and grated rind of 1 lemon
Freshly ground black pepper
450g (1 lb) rindless back bacon, diced
7-8 chirizo sausages, sliced
Olive oil for frying
Flat leaf parsley for garnish

In a saucepan, fry the onion and garlic in olive oil, add the green lentils, the juice and grated rind of the lemon and season with black pepper. Stir well and cook for 2 - 3 minutes. Add sufficient boiling water to cover and cook over a medium heat for 20 - 30 minutes until the lentils are tender, adding more water if necessary. When the lentils are cooked, blend them with the cooking liquid to a creamy consistency. Set aside.

In a separate pan, fry the bacon and sausage for 5 - 6 minutes. Return the lentils to a low heat and add the bacon and sausages. Season as necessary and cook for about 10 minutes.

Serve garnished with chopped parsley.

Fish

Fishing has always been important to Christchurch owing to its location between two rivers and near to the sea. Indeed it has been said that for centuries Christchurch thrived on contraband and fish!

Locally caught sea-fish such as turbot, sole, whiting, herring and mackerel and shellfish would have been on sale in the market place and they are also available in the area today. Oysters used to be very plentiful, a common shellfish eaten by anyone and not the delicacy they are now.

Our tastes in fish have changed over the years and our general preference is for the more 'meaty' types of fish such as cod, haddock and tuna as these recipes show.

Salmon and trout are still popular as fish to be served for special occasions. Fishing for them in this area has been carried out for centuries and the golden salmon on the top of Christchurch Priory denotes the fact that the Prior was always given the first salmon of the season to be caught in Christchurch Harbour.

Fishing is still a very popular sport in Christchurch.

Among the lobster pots at Stanpit, Christchurch Harbour

Steamed Salmon with Black Beans

Ken Hom

Serves 4

450g (1 lb) salmon fillet, boneless, skinned and divided into 4 equal pieces.
1 teaspoon salt
¼ teaspoon freshly ground white pepper
2 tablespoons black beans, rinsed and chopped
1½ tablespoons garlic, finely chopped
1 tablespoon fresh ginger, finely chopped
1½ tablespoons Shoaxing rice wine or dry sherry
1 tablespoon light soy sauce

Garnish

3 tablespoons spring onions, finely chopped
Small handful of fresh coriander
1½ tablespoons groundnut (peanut) oil

Sprinkle the salmon pieces evenly with the salt and pepper. Combine the black beans, garlic and ginger in a small bowl.

Put the fillets on a deep heatproof plate and evenly scatter the black bean mixture over the top. Pour the Shoaxing rice wine or dry sherry and soy sauce over the fish.

Set up a steamer or put a rack into a wok or deep pan and fill with 5 cm (2 in) of water. Bring the water to the boil over a high heat. Carefully lower the fish and plate into the steamer or on to the rack. Turn the heat to low and cover the pan or wok tightly. Steam gently for 8 - 10 minutes, depending on the thickness of the fillets. Top up with boiling water from time to time. When the fish is cooked, remove the plate from the steamer or wok. Scatter the spring onions and coriander on top of the fish.

Heat a wok or large frying pan until it is very hot. Add the oil and when it is very hot and slightly smoking, pour this over the fillets.

Serve at once.

Ragout of Monkfish with Pancetta, Dill, Tomatoes and Flageolet Beans

Eddie Blanchard
The Ship in Distress, Stanpit

Serves 4

1 x 1.2-1.5 kg. (2½-3 lb) monkfish tail
250g (9 oz) dried flageolets (soaked and cooked with pancetta rind)
115g (4 oz) diced pancetta
60g (2 oz) butter
2 beef tomatoes – skinned, seeded and chopped
Bunch of fresh dill, chopped with a few sprigs reserved
150ml (5 fl oz) double cream
600ml (1 pint) fish stock
60g (2 oz) butter, optional
Parmesan cheese, shavings
Salt and freshly ground pepper

Skin, fillet and strip sinew from monkfish, cut into half inch strips and season.

Sauté diced pancetta until lightly browned. Add flageolets and fish stock. Cook down until half the stock has been absorbed by beans. Stir in monkfish strips and simmer for 4 - 5 minutes. Add chopped dill, tomatoes and cream. Taste and season as necessary. Stir in the optional butter (if using it).

Warm all ingredients, but do not boil. Pile on to four plates.

Top with shaved Parmesan and springs of dill.

Braised Entrecôte of Cod
with Savoy Cabbage and Smoked Salmon

Eddie Blanchard
The Ship in Distress, Stanpit

Serves 4

4 x 200g (7 oz) equal size pieces thick cod fillet
115g (4 oz) butter
1 medium Savoy cabbage, cored and finely sliced
115g (4 oz) diced smoked salmon
150ml (5 fl oz) fish stock

Sea salt and freshly ground black pepper

Wash and dry the fish.

Melt 85g (3 oz) of the butter in a large saucepan. Add the cabbage and fry for 3 - 4 minutes. Stir in the stock and season with salt and pepper.

Lay the fish on the cabbage, dot with the remaining butter and bring to the boil. Cover and simmer for 12 - 15 minutes. Remove the fish, cover and keep warm. Raise the heat and reduce the cooking liquid until it lightly coats the cabbage. Stir in the smoked salmon and warm through.

To serve, spoon the cabbage and salmon on to four plates and top with the fish fillets.

Salmon in Puff Pastry
(En Croûte)

Pat Hicks

*A simple dish that never fails to impress your guests, whatever their age.
Delicious hot or cold, served with green salad and potato salad.*

Serves 4 generously

Tail of fresh Scottish Salmon approx. 675g (1½ lb)
Ask your fishmonger to skin and fillet it, so giving 2 pieces
1 x 450g (1 lb) packet frozen puff pastry, thawed
1 bunch of watercress, finely chopped
150ml (5 fl oz) tub of natural yoghurt, fromage fraîs or soured cream
Beaten egg, to brush

Grease a baking tray.

Roll out the puff pastry evenly on a floured board to make two rectangular shapes each, big enough to cover the salmon plus 2.5 cm (1 in) on all sides.

Place one piece of pastry on the prepared baking tray. Put one piece of the salmon, boned side up, on to the centre of the pastry and spread it with your choice of yoghurt, fromage fraîs or soured cream. Season lightly with salt and pepper. Place the watercress on top. Now spread the boned side of the second salmon fillet with yoghurt, fromage fraîs or soured cream and season lightly. Place this fillet, yoghurt side down on to the watercress.

Brush the four sides of the pastry with a little water and place the second piece of pastry on top. Press the two pieces of pastry together, trim to even the sides if necessary, leaving at least 2 cm (¾ in) then press together well and crimp the edges as you go. (It's easy to cut to a fish shape too).

Chill while preheating the oven to 200°C/400°F/Gas 6.

Brush the surface of the pastry well, not the cut edges, with beaten egg and bake for about 30 minutes, until golden, crisp and shiny.

If eating cold, leave to cool to firm the shape before slicing through with a sharp knife.

Baked Rainbow Trout

Dick Gill

Serves 2

    1 kg (2 lb) rainbow trout, gutted, head and tail removed
    ask you fishmonger to do this
    30g (1 oz) butter
    1 teaspoon lightly chopped mixed herbs, e.g. dill, parsley, chives, fennel, tarragon
    250ml (8 fl oz) dry white wine or cider

Pre-heat the oven to 190°C/375°F/Gas 5.

Wash the trout thoroughly in cold water, dry on absorbent kitchen towel. Put 2 x 7g (¼ oz) pieces of butter inside the trout belly, and sprinkle the inside with the herbs.

Take a large piece of kitchen foil and carefully lightly butter one side. It is most important not to make any holes or tears in the foil. Place the trout in the centre of the foil, turn up, fold and press the ends to form sides of a loose envelope. Pour in the wine at the open top, then fold, squeeze and press to completely seal.

Place the envelope on a baking tray and bake in the pre-heated oven for about 30 minutes (larger trout will require longer while smaller trout need only 20 - 25 minutes).

Remove from the oven and open the foil envelope <u>very carefully</u> from the top, there will be a risk of hot steam and hot liquid within. The skin of the fish can easily be removed by gently lifting with a blunt knife or spatula. Cut the fish along the lateral line and gently ease it off the bones.

Serve hot with the cooking juices poured over as a sauce. Garnish with a slice of lemon.

Alternatively this dish can be served cold with a salad.

Pan Fried Sea Bass with Crab and Coriander Ravioli, Chilli and Tomato Jam and Spring Onion Salsa

Jason Davenport, Head Chef
Splinters Restaurant

The crab used in our restaurant are landed at Poole, the sea bass within one kilometre from the Restaurant.
All other ingredients are natural/organic and sourced through local farms and suppliers wherever possible.

Serves 3

3 medium sized sea bass fillet, skin left on but scaled, cut into diagonal pieces
A little butter and oil to fry

Ravioli Pasta Dough

560g (1 lb 4 oz) fine Italian pasta flour
4 eggs
6 egg yolks
4 tablespoons extra virgin olive oil
Sea salt and ground black pepper

Ravioli Filling

115g (4 oz) white crab meat
60g (2 oz) dark crab meat
1 teaspoon fresh coriander leaves, chopped
A pinch of curry powder
Sea salt and ground black pepper
1 shallot, peeled and chopped

Salsa

3 spring onions, chopped
1 shallot, peeled and chopped
1 tomato, seeded, peeled and diced
1 red chilli pepper, diced
A squeeze of lemon juice
2 tablespoons extra virgin olive oil
1 teaspoon each coriander leaves, basil, chives, roughly chopped
A pinch of caster sugar
Sea salt and ground black pepper

<u>Tomato and Chilli Jam</u>

> 500g (18 oz) very ripe tomatoes
> 4 red chilli peppers, seeded and diced
> 4 cloves of garlic, peeled
> 5 cm (2 in) root ginger, peeled and roughly chopped
> 1 tablespoon Asian fish sauce (Nam Pla)
> 325g (11 oz) caster sugar
> 90ml (3 fl oz) red wine vinegar

To make the tomato and chilli jam: Using a liquidiser or blender process half of the tomatoes, the chillies, garlic, ginger and fish sauce to a fine purée. Put the purée, sugar and vinegar in a deep pot and slowly bring to the boil stirring all the time. When it reaches the boil, turn to a gentle simmer and add the remaining tomatoes, which should be diced. Skim off the foam and cook gently for 30 - 40 minutes, stirring every 5 minutes.

To make the ravioli: Combine all the ingredients in a food processor until the mixture comes together as course crumbs. Turn out on to a lightly floured surface and knead well to form a smooth ball of dough. (The mixture should be soft but not sticky). Roll out the pasta dough on the thinnest setting on a pasta machine. To make the ravioli, cut out twelve 9 cm (3½ in) circles.

To make the filling and fill the ravioli: Mix all the filling ingredients together. Using six of the circles put a ball of filling in the centre of each. Brush the edge of the circles with water and place the remaining circles on top. Press well to seal.

To make the salsa: Using a medium sized bowl mix the ingredients for the salsa.

To cook the ravioli: Bring a large pan of well salted ravioli to the boil and cook the ravioli for 4 - 5 minutes.

To prepare and cook the fish: Score the skin of the sea bass to prevent from curling. Season on both sides and lightly flour. Heat a little butter and oil in a in a non-stick pan and fry for approximately 2 - 3 minutes on each side.

To serve, place a little of the salsa in the middle of the plate, then place the two pieces of sea bass on top of this. Spoon a little of the warmed chilli jam on the top of the sea bass. This acts as a type of glue for the ravioli which you then sit on top.

Finish by spooning more chilli jam over the top of this. (The more fiery you like your food the more jam you should use!)

Millefeuille of Black Bream and Sweet Potato with a Prawn Salsa and a Warm Ginger Dressing

Rob Colmer
Café 39 at the Pines, Mudeford

Serves 2

4 x 90–120g (3-4 oz) fillets black bream
1 large sweet potato, peeled and thinly sliced
A little plain flour
A little oil and butter for frying
Chopped fresh chives to garnish
Salt and pepper

Prawn Salsa

½ medium onion
1 clove garlic, finely chopped
A pinch of mixed herbs
30ml (1 fl oz) dry white wine
½ seeded chopped chilli to taste
1 x 115g (4 oz) can peeled plum tomatoes, drained and chopped
½ tablespoon tomato purée
50g (1¾ oz) cooked, peeled prawns

Ginger Dressing

½ tablespoon Dijon mustard
150ml (5 fl oz) vegetable oil
1 teaspoon caster sugar
100g (3½ oz) root ginger, peeled and finely chopped
120ml (3¾ fl oz) rice vinegar

Heat the oil in deep fat fryer. Add the sweet potato and fry to light golden. Drain on absorbent kitchen paper towel and lightly sprinkle with salt and pepper. Set to one side.

To make the salsa: Heat a little oil in a thick-based pan, add the onion and sweat until transparent. Add the garlic, herbs and wine, reduce by half. Add the chilli and tomatoes. Simmer for 5 - 10 minutes stirring occasionally. Add the tomato purée, season to taste and add the prawns. Remove from the heat.

To make the ginger dressing: Place the Dijon mustard in a bowl and slowly add the oil, whisking constantly. Add the sugar, ginger and rice vinegar. Season to taste. To bring out the flavour of the ginger, gently warm the dressing over a small pan of hot water or in the microwave.

To cook the fish: Season the bream, lightly coat in flour. Pan fry on both sides in a little hot oil and butter, skin side down first. When cooked the flesh should be firm.

To assemble: Using two warm plates, put on two or three sweet potato 'crisps'. Place one bream fillet on top and spoon some prawn salsa on the fillet. Repeat with 'crisps', second fillet and prawn salsa, finishing with sweet potato crisps as the final layer. Drizzle the warm ginger dressing over the top and a little around the plate. Sprinkle with chives and serve with a steady hand so the layers remain intact.

Fish Poached with Shallots

Patricia Judge
Highcliffe Local History Society

Serves 4

450g (1 lb) white fish fillets
8 shallots
1 cup fish stock
2 tablespoons olive oil
1 tablespoon white wine vinegar
Fresh parsley, chopped

Chop the shallots and place them in a shallow dish. Arrange the fish fillets on top and pour over the stock and olive oil.

Poach till cooked, sprinkle with vinegar and chopped parsley and serve.

Steamed Sea Bass and Fresh Spinach with Cabernet Sauvignon Sauce

John Batchelor
Mudeford Fish Stall

Serves 4

5 bunches of spinach (about 1 kg (2 lb))
1.2 litres (2 pints) fish stock or water
4 sea bass fillets 175–225g (6-8 oz) each
60ml (2 fl oz) Cabernet Sauvignon
2 tablespoons red wine vinegar
3 medium shallots, minced
½ teaspoon salt
¼ teaspoon finely ground white pepper
225g (8 oz) unsalted butter, chilled and cut into small cubes

To prepare the spinach: Remove spinach stems and rinse leaves thoroughly. Chop leaves coarsely. Put spinach in a medium saucepan, cover and cook for 2 minutes over medium heat or until just wilted, but still green. Drain and keep warm.

To cook the fish: Pour stock or water into a medium saucepan with high sides or a steamer, place steamer rack in pan and heat liquid until simmering. Place fish fillets on rack and cover. Steam for 6 minutes or until just done (cooking time depends on thickness of fish). Test with a skewer, you should be able to penetrate fish easily. Cover fish and keep warm.

To prepare the sauce: In a small heavy saucepan, boil the wine and vinegar with shallots until about 2 tablespoons liquid remain. Add salt and white pepper. Over a low heat begin adding cubes of butter to the shallot mixture, whisking constantly, add butter 1 or 2 cubes at a time and wait until they are absorbed before adding more. The sauce should thicken, but butter should not melt. If pan begins to get very hot, remove it from heat and add some butter cubes off heat to cool sauce slightly. Remove from heat as soon as last butter cube is added. Strain the sauce if a smoother consistency is desired. Taste for seasoning. Keep warm.

To serve, place quarter of the spinach in the centre of each plate. Top with a fish fillet and serve Cabernet sauce over; serve remaining sauce separately.

This recipe is taken from the book "All About Fish" by John Batchelor.
Copies are available for £1 from The Fresh Fish Stall, Mudeford Quay.

Mackerel with Oranges

John Batchelor
Mudeford Fish Stall

Serves 4

4 medium sized mackerel

Marinade

150ml (5 fl oz) oil
150ml (5 fl oz) orange juice
A few drops of Tabasco, optional
Salt and freshly ground black pepper

Garnish

60g (2 oz) black olives
2 oranges, peeled and sliced

Clean, gut and wash the mackerel or ask your fishmonger to do this.

Make slanting incisions with a sharp knife across both sides of each fish. Place in a dish. Mix together the marinade ingredients and pour over the fish. Leave the fish to marinate for 2 hours, turning occasionally.

Drain the fish and place on a grill pan. Grill for 5-8 minutes on each side, brushing with the marinade.

When cooked, place on a serving dish, pour over the juices from the pan and serve garnished with orange slices and black olives.

Taken from the book "All About Fish" by John Batchelor.

Seafood Pie with Leeks and Blue Vinney

Richard Donaldson
T.W. Advertising

Serves 4

675g (1½ lb) floury potatoes such as Maris Piper
450g (1 lb) cod, haddock, whiting or coley fillet
225g (8 oz) peeled prawns
175ml (6 fl oz) milk
350g (12 oz) leeks
30g (1 oz) butter
Freshly grated nutmeg
Salt and pepper

Sauce

60g (2 oz) butter
3 tablespoons plain white flour
175ml (6 fl oz) milk
115g (4 oz) Dorset Blue Vinney (or Stilton)
4 tablespoons single cream
A pinch of cayenne pepper

Bring a medium saucepan of salted water to the boil, add the potato slices. Cook for 5 - 7 minutes until partially softened. Drain.

Meanwhile place the fish in a shallow pan, pour over 175 ml (6 fl oz) of milk, season lightly and poach for about 5 minutes until the fish flakes easily. Drain, reserving the juices, and flake all of the fish.

Trim and slice the leeks. Melt the 30g (1 oz) of butter in a pan and gently fry the leeks for 3 minutes until softened, adding freshly grated nutmeg. Set aside to cool.

Lightly butter a 3 pint pie dish.

Pre-heat the oven to 190°C/375°F/Gas 5.

To make the sauce, in a small saucepan melt the 60g (2 oz) of butter, add the flour and cook, stirring for 1 minute. Remove from the heat and gradually blend in the milk and reserved juices from the fish poaching. Return to the heat and cook, stirring continuously, until thickened. Crumble in the cheese, adding the cream and pepper, stirring until incorporated and smooth.

Mix together the fish, prawns and leeks in the prepared pie dish. Spoon half of the cheese sauce over this mixture, then layer the potatoes over this filling. Pour the remaining sauce over the potatoes.

Place on a baking sheet and cook in the oven for 45 - 50 minutes until bubbling and golden.

Moules Mariniere

Jamie Treadwell
The Thomas Tripp, Christchurch

Serves 4

1 onion, chopped
3 cloves garlic, chopped
300ml (10 fl oz) dry white wine
2¾ kg (6 lb) prepared mussels
Mixed herbs
1 litre (1¾ pints) double cream
Oil for frying

In a large wok fry the onion and garlic. Add the wine and cook for 3 minutes. Add the mussels and then the cream, cover the wok with a lid and cook for about 8 - 10 minutes.

Add the mixed herbs and cook for a final 2 minutes.

Salmon and Dill Savoury Pancakes

Julie Stanley
Suzettes Pancake House, Christchurch

Serves 4

425ml (15 fl oz) pancake batter mixture
Juice of a lemon
Oil for frying
4 salmon finger fillets
300ml (10 fl oz) milk
60g (2 oz) butter
30g (1 oz) soft cream cheese
1 tablespoon flour
Salt and pepper
75ml (2½ fl oz) double cream
Fresh dill
Lemon wedges and dill leaves for garnishing

Sprinkle salmon fillets with salt and pepper, lemon juice and knob of butter. Place on a microwaveable plate and cover with cling film. Cook in a 800w microwave oven on full power for 5 - 6 minutes until light pink in colour and the skin comes away from the fillet easily.

Make four 25 cm (10 in) pancakes. Separating the pancakes with greaseproof paper, pile them up and keep them warm in a low temperature oven.

Melt the remaining butter in a pan, remove from the heat, then add the flour and season with salt and pepper. Stir to make a roux then slowly add the milk. Return the pan to the heat and bring back to the boil, stirring the sauce all the time until it thickens. Add the cream cheese and fresh dill and continue to simmer for a further 10 minutes, adjusting the seasoning as necessary. Then stir in the cream.

Place the prepared pancakes on individual plates and lay a salmon fillet along the centre of pancake. Pour the dill sauce over the salmon and fold the two sides of the pancake in to overlap.

Garnish with a wedge of lemon and dill leaves.

Serve with a green salad and warm, buttered French bread.

Cod Fish Cakes

Paul Leccacorvi
Captain Cod, Christchurch

Serves 4

450g (1 lb) Maris Piper potatoes
225g (8 oz) cod fillet
60g (2 oz) butter
Bunch of fresh parsley
Salt and pepper
Oil for frying
Lemon wedges and parsley to decorate

Peel the potatoes and cut into 2.5 cm (1 in) pieces. Boil in plenty of salted water for 6 - 8 minutes until cooked through, but not mushy. Mash the potato adding the butter and seasoning to taste. Chop the parsley and add to the mashed potato.

Lightly season the cod fillet with salt and pepper, place on a microwaveable plate and cover with cling film. Cook in a 800w microwave oven on full power for 5 - 6 minutes until the flesh of the fish flakes easily.

Mix (but do not over mix) the flaked fish with the potato mixture. Using an ice-cream scoop, remove a portion of the mixture and flatten to a 1 cm (½ in) thick disc, continue until all the mixture is used. The fish cakes should be refrigerated for at least 30 minutes before cooking. They can be frozen at this stage.

Shallow fry the fish cakes in the oil for 3 - 4 minutes each side until golden brown. Garnish with a wedge of lemon and parsley.

Alternatively, the frozen fish cakes, once thawed, can be deep fried. While heating the oil to 160 170°C, dust them in flour and coat in batter letting any excess batter drip away.

Ensure that the batter is cold.

Gently lower the fish cakes into the deep fat fryer and cook them for 7 - 8 minutes until they are golden brown.

Drain and enjoy your fish cakes.

Savoury Tuna

Zoë Martin

Serves 4

1 large tin of tuna
1 onion, chopped finely
1 pepper, chopped (red or green)
Oil for frying
60g (2 oz) butter
1 tablespoon flour
300ml (10 fl oz) milk
60g (2 oz) Cheddar cheese, grated
60g (2 oz) mushrooms, sliced
Salt and pepper

Lemon wedges, tomato slices or parsley to decorate

Fry the onion and pepper in a little oil until cooked through and softened.

Open the tin of tuna, drain the liquid and flake the fish.

Melt the butter in a pan, remove from the heat, then add the flour and season with salt and pepper. Stir to make a roux then slowly add the milk. Return the pan to the heat and bring back to the boil, stirring the sauce all the time until it thickens. Add the cheese, continue to simmer for a further 10 minutes, adjust the seasoning as required. Do not allow the sauce to become too thick, add more liquid if necessary.

Remove from the heat, add the flaked tuna, pepper and onion mixture and the sliced mushrooms. Mix, test for taste and adjust seasoning as necessary.

Garnish with a wedge of lemon and dill leaves.

Serve with rice or pasta.

Gratin of Seafood

Betty Peters

Serves 4

> 560g (1¼ lb) cod fillet, cut into small strips
> 60g (2 oz) button mushrooms, sliced
> 115g (4 oz) peeled prawns
> 145g (5 oz) Parmesan cheese, grated
> Juice of ½ large lemon

Sauce

> 300ml (10 fl oz) milk
> 6 peppercorns
> A blade of mace
> A slice of onion
> 30g (1 oz) flour
> 30g (1 oz) butter
> Salt and pepper

Pre-heat the oven to 180°C/350°F/Gas 4.

Butter 4 individual gratin dishes. Divide the fish, prawns and mushrooms between the dishes, sprinkling with lemon juice.

To make the sauce, put the milk in a saucepan with the onion slice, peppercorns and mace and warm for 15 minutes allowing the flavourings to infuse in the milk. Strain and discard the spices and onion.

In a separate saucepan, melt the butter, add the flour and make a roux. Over a low heat, gradually add the flavoured milk, stirring continuously until thick. Add salt and pepper to taste.

Spoon the sauce over the fish, then sprinkle generously with Parmesan cheese. Bake in the oven for 20 - 25 minutes until brown.

Cheesy Fishes

Gill Taylor

Serves 4

450g (1 lb) white fish
60g (2 oz) frozen peas
450g (1 lb) potatoes
½ onion, chopped finely
30g (1 oz) Cheddar cheese, grated
115g (4 oz) wholemeal breadcrumbs
A large pinch of dried parsley
Salt and pepper
1 tablespoon flour
Oil for frying

Cheese Sauce

150ml (5 fl oz) milk
1 teaspoon cornflour
30g (1 oz) butter
60g (2 oz) Cheddar cheese, grated

Poach the fish in ½ pint of water until tender. Allow to cool, then flake the fish, removing any bones. Reserve the cooking liquid.

Cook the frozen peas in boiling water for 2 minutes, then drain and add to the fish. Peel the potatoes and cut into small pieces. Boil the potatoes in the reserved fish stock until tender, drain and then mash. Gently fry the onion in a little oil until soft.

To make the cheese sauce, melt the butter in a saucepan, add the cornflour and make a roux. Over a low heat, gradually add the milk, stirring continuously until thick. Add the cheese and mix thoroughly for 2 - 3 minutes.

In a large bowl, combine all the prepared ingredients and the parsley, stirring well. Place the mixture on a floured surface, divide into 8 and make fish shapes (either by hand or using a cutter). Place the shapes on an oiled baking tray and sprinkle with the remaining Cheddar cheese. Grill under a medium/high heat until the shapes are hot and browned on top (about 8 - 10 minutes).

Serve either on their own or as part of a main meal.

Tuna and Cucumber Quiche

Jane Lawley FIHEc
Head of Home Economics
Homefield School

Serves 4

20 cm (8 in) prepared shortcrust pastry case
175g (6 oz) tin of tuna
¼ - ½ cucumber, sliced (but not peeled)
150ml (5 fl oz) milk
2 eggs
15g (½ oz) Cheddar cheese, grated
A pinch of Cayenne pepper
Salt and pepper

In a large bowl, beat the eggs, milk and seasoning together.

Open the tin of tuna, drain the liquid and flake the fish.

Spread the fish over the base of the prepared pastry case, arrange the cucumber slices over the fish overlapping the slices.

Pour the egg mixture over the flan filling and sprinkle the grated cheese over the top.

Cook in a pre-heated oven 180°C/350°F/Gas 4 for 25 - 30 minutes.

Alternatively cook in a 800w microwave on full power for 5½ minutes until the centre of the flan is set, but not dry. (Check after 4 minutes).

Leave to stand for 5 - 10 minutes

Serve hot or cold.

This dish freezes well.

Roasted Monkfish and Lobster
with Roasted Garlic and a Rosemary Jus

The Chewton Glen
New Milton, Hampshire

Serves 4

4 x 175g (6 oz) monkfish portions
1 carrot, cut into strips and lightly cooked
1 leek, cut into strips and lightly cooked
1 courgette, cut into strips and lightly cooked
1 large celeriac, cut into strips and lightly cooked
4 cloves of garlic
225g (8 oz) lobster per person, cooked and allowed to cool

Sauce

175g (6 oz) chicken winglets, bones
½ carrot
½ onion
A stick of celery
½ leek
1 bay leaf
A sprig of thyme
10 white peppercorns
250ml (8½ fl oz) reduced veal stock
250ml (8½ fl oz) chicken stock
250ml (8½ fl oz) white wine
125g (4½ oz) butter
4 sprigs of rosemary
Salt and freshly ground pepper

Additional rosemary sprigs, for garnish

To make the sauce: In a very large pot, brown the chicken winglets/bones lightly in a little oil with the vegetables, add the peppercorns, herbs (but not the rosemary) and the wine. Reduce the wine by half, then add the veal and chicken stock. Simmer gently for one hour.

Skim off any fat from the top and pass the sauce through a sieve. Return the sauce to the heat and boil to reduce to a very light coating consistency. Add half the rosemary and the butter, season as necessary with salt and pepper and simmer for a further 5 minutes. Again, pass the sauce through a sieve.

To assemble the dish: Seal the monkfish in a hot frying pan with a little olive oil, adding the remaining rosemary and garlic. Then roast in a pre-heated oven 220°C/425°F/Gas 7 for approximately five minutes.

Re-boil the sauce, placing the cooked lobster in the pan to re-heat with the sauce.

Re-heat the julienne of vegetables in a little water and butter, salt and pepper.

On a large plate, arrange the vegetables in a pile with the lobster. Place the monkfish and garlic at the side and pour the sauce carefully around. Garnish with sprigs of rosemary and roasted garlic from the sauce.

Chilli Fish

Yas Maybank
The Grosvenor Lodge Guest House

Serves 4

2 tablespoons butter
1 teaspoon hot chilli powder
2 medium onions, finely chopped
1 clove garlic, crushed in a little salt
600ml (1 pint) chicken stock
400g (14 oz) can of tomatoes
2 tablespoons tomato purée
Juice of 1 lemon
2 teaspoons clear honey

450g (1 lb) haddock fillet, skinned and cut into 2.5 cm (1 in) pieces
225g (8 oz) smoked haddock fillet as above
Salt and pepper

Melt butter in a sauté pan or large saucepan. Add chilli powder and cook over a low heat for 1 minute. Add the onions and garlic and fry for 3 minutes. Stir in stock, tomatoes, tomato purée, lemon and honey. Cover and simmer for 30 minutes, or until quite thick.

Add the fish and simmer for 10 minutes. Season with salt and pepper.

Serve with boiled rice and a crisp green salad.

For a variation: Substitute 225g (8 oz) of peeled cooked prawns for 225g (8 oz) of the fish. To avoid over-cooking add the prawns 5 minutes after the fish has been added.

Spicy Grilled Crab Meat

The Boathouse
Quomps, Christchurch

Serves 2

1 clove of garlic, finely chopped
1 white onion, grated
A bunch of coriander, finely chopped
A bunch of flat leaf parsley, finely chopped
Olive oil for frying
450g (1 lb) white crab meat
Juice and grated rind of 1 lime
400g (14 oz) can of tomato purée
2 tablespoons coconut milk or grated creamed coconut
Parmesan cheese, grated

Fry the onion, garlic and herbs in a little olive oil until the onion is golden. Add the crab meat, lime juice and grated rind and cook for 2 - 3 minutes. Add the tomato and coconut milk and continue to cook until the juices have reduced and thickened.

Fill a gratin dish or a prepared crab shell with the mixture and top with freshly grated Parmesan cheese. Grill until golden brown.

Meat & Poultry

Christchurch has always had a wide range of meat to offer. In the past cattle, sheep and goats would have been kept on the manorial estates to provide beef, veal, mutton and lamb as well as milk. The breeding stock and animals giving milk would have been kept over the winter when their food was scarce. The other animals would be killed in the autumn and the meat salted to preserve it for use during the winter months.

Domesticated birds such as geese, ducks, chickens and pigeons were also kept so that their meat was available all year round. Wild fowl and small birds were also used in dishes.

People who were fortunate to have their own land could grow corn and keep chickens. Pigs were also kept and their meat was smoked rather than salted for later consumption as ham or bacon.

Poaching, of hares and rabbits for example, has always been carried out. However, the hunting of game was the prerogative of royalty and the gentry and was forbidden for the ordinary people, as was fishing in the harbour, if they did not have the rights to do so. Being caught red-handed (with the animal's blood on their hands) was a punishable offence, severely so in the case of taking deer - the punishment was death!

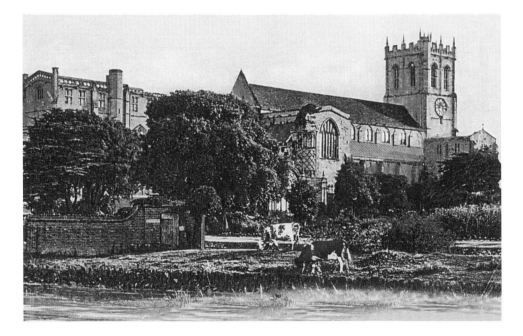

Cows grazing around Christchurch Priory 1905

Chicken with Pine Nuts and Red Pepper

Marguerite Patten

Serves 2

1 red pepper
Salt and freshly ground black pepper
A pinch of chilli powder or Cayenne pepper, optional
1 tablespoon plain flour
2 chicken breasts
1 tablespoon sunflower oil
2 tablespoons sliced spring onions
1 teaspoon chopped tarragon
1 teaspoon Dijon mustard
2 tablespoons pine nuts
200 ml (7 fl oz) crème fraîche

<u>Garnish</u>

Chopped tarragon
1 tablespoon pine nuts

Halve and de-seed the pepper, put under a preheated grill until the skins turn black then place in a plastic bag until cool, strip away the skin and cut the flesh into narrow strips.

Blend the seasonings with the flour and coat the chicken. Heat the oil in the frying pan and cook the chicken until golden brown and almost tender. Add the onions and stir over the heat for several minutes or until golden in colour, put in nearly all the pepper strips, the tarragon, mustard, pine nuts and lastly the creme fraîche, heat for a few minutes.

Serve topped with the remaining strips of red pepper, tarragon and pine nuts.

Quick Lamb Casserole

Carol King

A recipe for busy housewives and Mums, that is ready to serve from the oven as a meal in itself.

Serves 4

4 lamb shoulder chops, trimmed
1 small onion, peeled and sliced
1 x 300g (11 oz) can sliced carrots, drained
1 x 300g (11 oz) can garden peas, drained
1 tablespoon pearl barley
Prepared gravy, e.g. Bisto
2 medium potatoes, peeled and sliced
Oil for frying

Pre-heat the oven to 220°C/425°F/Gas 7.

Fry the shoulder chops on both sides to seal. Place them in a large casserole dish or oven-proof roasting dish. Gently fry the onion in a little hot oil until soft, then add to the chops in the casserole. Add the carrots and peas. Then sprinkle the pearl barley over them.

Cover the meat and vegetables with potatoes to form a 'lid'. Pour on enough gravy to cover the meat and vegetables. Bake for approximately one hour or until the potatoes are brown and crisp.

Beef Patties

A favourite nourishing family meal which is easy to prepare.

Serves 2

400g (14 oz) fresh minced beef
A little plain flour
1 small onion, peeled and sliced
1 x 400g (14 oz) can whole plum tomatoes
Salt and freshly ground pepper
Prepared gravy, e.g. Bisto
Oil for frying

Pre-heat the oven to 200°C/400°F/Gas 6.

On a lightly floured surface shape the minced beef into 8 small round, flat patties (like beefburgers). Shallow fry them quickly in a little hot oil to seal them on both sides, remove and drain briefly on crumpled kitchen towels if wished. Place the patties into a large casserole dish or oven-proof roasting dish.

Fry the onion in a little oil until soft. Place the onion around the patties in the dish followed by the tomatoes. Lightly season with salt and pepper. Pour on enough prepared gravy to cover the meat. Place on the middle shelf of the pre-heated oven and cook for 45 minutes.

Ideally served with mashed potatoes and green vegetables of your choice.

Chicken in Orange

Barbara Hamilton Sarmiento

Serves 4 - 6

8 fresh chicken thighs
3 teaspoons English mustard powder
3 tablespoons brown sugar
300ml (10 fl oz) fresh orange juice
2 teaspoons lemon juice
Salt to taste.

Skin the chicken thighs, put into a shallow oven-proof dish. Using a small bowl mix the mustard, sugar, orange juice, lemon juice and salt. Pour this mixture over the chicken, cover and leave to marinate in a cool place for 5 - 6 hours.

Pre-heat the oven to 200°C/400°F/Gas 6 and put in the dish of chicken with its marinade.

Cook, turning occasionally, for about 1 hour until the marinade has caramelised to a sticky golden brown.

Marinated Pork Fillet Glazed with Marsala on a Bed of Spinach and Watercress in a Minted Raspberry and Walnut Dressing

Mary and Bruce Golding-Cooney

Serves 4

4 small or 2 large pork fillets/tenderloins
145g (5 oz) washed baby leaf spinach, stalks removed
145g (5 oz) washed watercress leaves, stalks removed
2 tablespoons cooking oil of your choice
175ml (6 fl oz) Italian Marsala wine
Salt and freshly ground black pepper

Dry Marinade

1 teaspoon black pepper
1 teaspoon chopped fresh thyme
1 teaspoon chopped fresh sage
1 large bay leaf, chopped
½ teaspoon allspice
2 cloves garlic, crushed or finely chopped.

Dressing

1 tablespoon raspberry vinegar infused previously with 2-3 sprigs of fresh mint
3 tablespoons walnut oil.

Garnish

A few sprigs of mint and watercress

Trim away any shiny skin or sinew from the pork fillets.

Mix together the ingredients for the dry marinade and coat the fillets with it. Leave overnight in the refrigerator. Scrape off the marinade and cut the pork into medallions. Heat the oil in a shallow pan, add the meat and brown it on all sides, season then add the Marsala. Turn up the heat and reduce the liquid until it forms a glaze on the meat.

Mix together the spinach and watercress leaves, arrange in the centre of a plate.

To make the dressing: Mix together the strained raspberry vinegar and the walnut oil. Season with salt and pepper. Drizzle on and around the bed of leaves.

To serve, arrange the pork fillet on the dressed bed of leaves. Garnish with sprigs of mint or watercress.

Quick Beef Stroganoff

Norma Fox

Serves 4

500g (1 lb) stewing steak, trimmed and cubed
1 large onions, sliced into rings
1 tin condensed mushroom soup
1 packet savoury beef soup (dry)
200ml (7 fl oz) sweet sherry
1 clove garlic crushed (optional)

Place all the ingredients in a large casserole.

Mix well, then place in a low oven 140°C/275°F/Gas 1 for 4 hours.

Serve with boiled rice.

Cream may be added just before serving.

Doreen's Duck
(With Help From a Friend)

Doreen Davies

Serves 4

4 duck breasts
A little honey to glaze
2 large potatoes, peeled
Oil and butter for frying
50ml (1¾ fl oz) Madeira

Sauce

100ml (3½ fl oz) Madeira
1 tablespoon honey
1 tablespoon dark soy sauce
1 teaspoon five-spice powder

Place all the sauce ingredients into a saucepan, bring to the boil then simmer slowly and allow to reduce by one third.

Par-cook the potatoes by bringing to the boil and then simmering for 8 minutes. Remove and drain off the water and keep to one side.

Pre-heat the oven to 200-220°C/400-425°F/Gas 6-7.

Prick or score the duck skin to release fat during cooking. Place the duck in a shallow roasting pan and cook in the oven for 30 - 45 minutes depending on your preference for pink or well done. Fifteen minutes before the duck is ready, remove from the oven, tip off the fat, brush the skins with honey and return to the oven to finish cooking and to glaze.

Remove the duck from the roasting tin and pour the Madeira into the tin. Stir to dissolve the sticky duck juice residue, add the sauce and bring back to the boil.

To make the rosti: Grate the potatoes add salt and divide into four about the size of a duck breast. Shallow fry in a mixture of hot oil and butter on medium heat, shaping, as each one goes into the pan. Cook them slowly, turning as necessary until tender and golden then turn up the heat to brown and crisp them.

To serve, place a rosti on each warm plate, slice the duck breasts and arrange along each rosti to overlap it on one side, then strain the sauce over.

An ideal accompaniment is a stir fry of sliced leeks and mange-tout with a little soy sauce added. Stir in some strips of cucumber at the very end to warm through, but keep them crisp.

Sausage Creole

Norma Fox

Serves 4

> 450g (1 lb) sausage meat
> 225g (8 oz) sliced onions
> 450g (1 lb) sliced apples
> 225g (8 oz) long grain rice
> 1 large tin tomatoes
> Salt and freshly ground black pepper
> Dry mixed herbs

Pre-heat the oven to 180°C/350°F/Gas 3.

Layer the sausage meat, onion, apple, rice and tomatoes in a casserole in that order.

Season with salt, pepper and mixed herbs to taste.

Cook in the oven for 1½ hours.

Cover the casserole for the first hour only.

Turkey Skewers
with Tomato and Olive Salsa

Mary Reader
Reader Communications

Serves 2

2 cloves of garlic, crushed
60ml (2 fl oz) lemon juice
1 tablespoon fresh oregano, chopped
1 tablespoon olive oil
Salt and freshly ground pepper
225g (8 oz) turkey breast, cubed
1 small red pepper, seeded and cut into 2 cm (1 in) cubes
3 fresh bay leaves

Tomato & Olive Salsa

85g (3 oz) mixed green and black olives, pitted and finely chopped
1 small red onion, chopped
2 plum tomatoes, finely chopped
1 tablespoon olive oil
Salt and pepper

In a shallow dish, mix together the garlic, lemon juice, oregano, olive oil and salt and pepper. Add the turkey and mix well. Leave in a cool place to marinade for 2 hours.

Meanwhile to prepare the salsa, put the olives, onion, tomatoes and olive oil in a bowl and mix together well. Season with salt and pepper as necessary, then chill until required.

Remove the turkey from the marinade and thread on to skewers, adding the pepper and bay leaves at regular intervals. Pre-heat the grill, then place the skewers on a grill pan with a rack and grill, turning occasionally, for about 10 minutes until the turkey is thoroughly cooked.

Serve on a bed of rice with the salsa.

Opposite: *Turkey Skewers with Tomato and Olive Salsa*
Next page: *Thai Prawns in Coconut (see p.33)*

Pollo Granadina
(Chicken Granada Style)

Sanchos Spanish Restaurant and Tapas

Serves 4 - 5

100ml (3½ fl oz) olive oil
6 cloves garlic, peeled
1 x 1.75-2 kg (3½ - 4 lb) fresh chicken, jointed
200g (7 oz) Serrano ham, diced
50ml (1¾ fl oz) medium sherry
50ml (1¾ fl oz) brandy
Salt and pepper
A little chopped fresh parsley

Heat the olive oil in a large frying pan, add the whole garlic cloves and fry until golden. Remove the garlic and reserve. Add the chicken joints to the pan and fry for about 10 minutes, turning occasionally, until nicely brown on all sides. Add the Serrano ham to the pan and cook for 2 - 3 minutes.

Add the sherry, brandy, the reserved browned garlic and season with salt and pepper. Cover and simmer for about 25 minutes or until the chicken is tender.

Serve sprinkled with the parsley and with hot freshly made potato chips to accompany.

Previous page: *Beef Medallions with Stilton Sauce (see p.102)*
Opposite: *Pan Fried Sea Bass with Crab and Coriander Ravioli (see p.50)*

Lemon Marinated Rabbit

Ian Naughton, Sous Chef
Pommery's, Christchurch

A delicious flavoured rabbit recipe that needs to be prepared the day before.

Serves 4

2 rabbits
2 large potatoes, peeled
Olive oil
400g (14 oz) sugar snap peas, stringed
1 tablespoon flat parsley leaves, shredded
Salt and pepper

Marinade

Juice of 4 lemons
1 bunch approx. 15g (½ oz) thyme sprigs
200ml (7 fl oz) dry white wine
Salt and pepper

Sauce

A little oil or butter
1 onion, finely chopped
100ml (3½ fl oz) dry white wine
300ml (10 fl oz) water
2 teaspoons redcurrant jelly

Portion the rabbits or ask the butcher to do it. Cut off the back legs, front legs and then cut the saddle in two. Trim and keep all trimmings. Place the front legs and trimmings on a plate, cover with cling film, refrigerate.

To marinate the serving portions: Put the back leg and saddle portions in a bowl, mix together the marinade ingredients and pour over. Cover with the cling film and refrigerate overnight.

To make the sauce: Cut the trimmings and front legs into small pieces removing any offal and obvious fat. Using a sauté pan heat a little oil or butter quickly and fry the pieces to brown. Add the onion and sweat for a few minutes on a low heat. Add the wine, water and stir in the red currant jelly. Simmer uncovered for one hour until the liquid is reduced to a syrupy coating consistency. Add extra water if the sauce reduces too quickly. Strain through a sieve into a small pan, and keep to one side.

To cook the potatoes: Pre-heat the oven to 200°C/400°F/Gas 6.
Slice the potatoes into 2 cm (¾ in) thick rounds, brush with olive oil and season with salt and pepper. Place them flat on a baking tray. Bake in oven for 20 - 30 minutes until golden brown and soft in the centre.

To cook the rabbit: Heat a frying or griddle pan. Remove the rabbit from the marinade and sear both sides on the pan. Finish cooking in the hot oven for 10 minutes.

To serve, re-heat the sauce, add in the sugar snap peas to cook for 2 minutes.

Using four warm plates, place potato slices in the centre of each. Divide the rabbit between the plates, stacking on the potato, spoon the sauce and sugar snap peas over and then sprinkle with flat parsley.

Note: Add a little strained marinade to the sauce if you want a sharper flavour.

Roasted Loin of Lamb
Served with Pancetta Rosti, Celeriac Mousse
And Redcurrant Mint Jus

Kevin Brown, Head Chef
The Lord Bute, Highcliffe

Serves 2

1 best end neck (rack) of lamb-fillet with 6-7 bones.
Ask your butcher to remove the 'eye' or long fillet and trim.
A little oil and butter for frying
Salt and pepper

Pancetta Rosti

2 medium potatoes, peeled and grated.
60g (2 oz) pancetta
30g (1 oz) chopped fresh parsley
1 egg yolk
A little oil and butter

Celeriac Mousse

1 medium celeriac, peeled to give approximately 350g (12 oz)
A few drops of lemon juice
1 egg yolk
60-90ml (2-3 fl oz) cream.

Redcurrant Mint Jus

600ml (1 pint) good brown stock reduced to 150 ml (5 fl oz)
2 tablespoons redcurrant jelly
100ml (3½ fl oz) dry white wine
Fresh mint, finely chopped.

Have ready 2 x 10 cm (4 in) round metal rings and a baking tray.
Pre-heat the oven to 180°C/350°F/Gas 4.

To make the rosti: Mix all the ingredients together and season with salt and pepper. Heat the oil and butter in a frying pan, place the metal rings in and place half the rosti mixture in each. Fry to golden brown, turn over and brown the second side. Lift the rosti on to a baking tray and remove the rings. Bake in the pre-heated oven for approximately 15 minutes or until tender.

For the celeriac mousse : Simmer the celeriac until tender in lightly salted water with lemon juice. Drain thoroughly, then purée in a food processor or mixer. Add the egg yolk, cream and season to taste. Place in a bowl, cover and leave to one side.

Make the jus: In a small pan bring the reduced stock to the boil. Add the redcurrant jelly stirring to melt it. Add the wine and continue cooking until the jus has reduced a little. Add mint and season.

To cook the lamb: Turn the oven up to 210°C/415°F/Gas 6 - 7.
Fry the lamb in a little hot oil and butter to seal the surface. Place in the hot oven for 6-10 minutes, depending on how you like your lamb cooked through. Remove and allow it to rest for a few minutes. Re-heat the rosti and celeriac, if necessary.

To serve, place each rosti on a plate, place a spoon of celeriac on top. Slice the lamb and place on the celeriac, overlapping and building upwards. Coat with the jus and garnish with a sprig of mint or rosemary.

Accompany this with some fine beans tossed in butter.

Savoury Sausagemeat Slice

A. Weir
Portfield School

Serves 8

900g (2 lb) sausage meat
450g (1 lb) onions, finely chopped
2 teaspoons mixed herbs
225g (8 oz) mushrooms, sliced
3 cloves garlic, finely chopped
Oil for frying

<u>Pastry</u>

450g (1 lb) self-raising flour
225g (8 oz) margarine
Beaten egg

Pre-heat the oven to 200°C/400°F/Gas 6.

Place the flour and margarine in a mixing bowl, mix together until the margarine is fully incorporated into the flour, add a little boiling water until a dough forms. When the pastry is cool, divide into two and roll half into an oblong shape 15 cm x 40 cm (6 in x 15 in).

For the filling, put the onion and garlic in a saucepan with a little oil and fry for about 5 minutes, add the mushrooms and mixed herbs and fry for a further 10 minutes. Strain the mixture and allow to cool. Mix the cooled mixture with the raw sausage meat, then spread over the rolled-out pastry, leaving a 2.5 cm (1 in) border all round. Brush the border with beaten egg, then roll out the remaining half of the pastry to cover the filling, seal the edges. Brush the pastry with the remaining beaten egg and place in the pre-heated oven for about 45 minutes until golden brown.

To serve, cut into slices 2.5 cm (1 in) thick and serve either hot with potatoes and vegetables or cold with a salad. Using puff pastry will create a lighter effect.

Christmas Lamb

Anne Wilkinson
Christchurch Council

Serves 4 – 6

1 x 2½-3 kg (5-6 lb) leg of Dorset lamb
A little vegetable oil
3 or 4 fat cloves of garlic, crushed
1 teaspoon roughly crushed black peppercorns
Fresh rosemary sprigs.

Mulled Wine - to prepare the night before

1 bottle red wine
2 mulled wine spice bags
or
your own combination of juniper berries, allspice, cinnamon, nutmeg, cloves, etc.

To mull the wine: Heat the wine gently on the hob with the spices for 20 minutes, do not boil. Remove from the heat and leave to cool overnight. Discard the spice bag or strain out loose spices.

Next day, have ready a deep heavy roasting tin with a lid (or use foil if no lid available). Pre-heat the oven to 230°C/450°F/Gas 8.

To cook the lamb: Place a little oil into the roasting tin and heat on top of the hob. Add the garlic and black pepper, fry until the garlic begins to colour. Place the lamb in the tin and roast in the oven, uncovered, for 30 minutes. Remove the tin from the oven, reduce the temperature to 170°C/325°F/Gas 3. Spoon off excess fat, leaving the dark meat juices. Add the mulled wine and rosemary.

Place the tin on the hob on a high heat until the wine begins to bubble. Baste the meat with the wine, cover with the lid, or foil pressed around well to seal, and return to the oven for 1½ hours basting once or twice.

Remove the lamb to a carving dish, cover and keep warm. (The sauce should be lightly syrupy, so if it is a little runny boil it briskly in an uncovered pan to reduce it. If there is not enough, add a little wine or dry sherry). This recipe is good served with potato and parsnip mash made with the addition of plenty of butter, cream and a pinch of nutmeg.

Fricassée of Wild Boar

Richard Donaldson
T.W. Advertising

Serves 6

2 kg (4 lb) wild boar, cut into bite-size chunks
50ml (2 fl oz) Calvados
425ml (15 fl oz) red wine
150ml (5 fl oz) double cream
3 tablespoons olive oil
30g (1 oz) butter

Marinade

100g (3½ oz) onions, sliced
1 carrot, sliced
2 cloves garlic
Bouquet Garni (thyme, bayleaf, rosemary, parsley and sage)
A pinch of Cayenne pepper
1 teaspoon sea salt
Black pepper
1 litre (1¾ pints) red wine
50ml (2 fl oz) Calvados
50ml (2 fl oz) cider vinegar
90ml (3 fl oz) olive oil (or walnut oil)

Place the diced meat in a large (non-metallic) bowl with all of the marinade ingredients, adding the oil last. Leave to marinate at room temperature for 24 hours, turning occasionally.

Remove the meat, pat dry on absorbent paper, reserving the marinade. In a large heavy-bottomed casserole, sauté the meat in the oil and butter until browned, de-glaze the pan with the Calvados and flame. Add the wine together with an equal amount of the strained marinade to cover the meat. Purée all the herbs and vegetables from the marinade and add to the dish, cover and then cook in a pre-heated oven 180°C/350°F/Gas 4 for 1¼ - 1½ hours, adding more wine if this seems necessary.

Remove the meat and keep warm on a serving dish. Add the cream to the sauce and stir over a low heat. Pour the sauce over the meat just before serving.

This dish can also be made with cubed leg of pork, but increase the length of marinating from 24 to 48 hours.

Kleftiko
(Baked Lamb with Oregano)

Chris Panaretou
Christopher Mark Hairdressing, Christchurch

Serves 6

1.5-1.8kg (3-4 lb) portions of lamb (shoulder) with the bone left in
1 bayleaf
2 sticks of cinnamon
4-5 whole cloves
1 level tablespoon of oregano
1 sliced onion
375ml (13 fl oz) water
Salt and freshly ground black pepper

Pre-heat oven to 220°C/425°F/Gas 7.

Remove any excess fat from the lamb, wash it and dry it, then place into a large casserole dish with a tight fitting lid.

Add the bayleaf, cinnamon, cloves and sprinkle over the oregano. Season with salt and pepper. Place the onions on top of the lamb and pour over the water. Cover with the lid and bake in the oven for approximately 3 hours or until tender and the meat literally falls off the bone.

Serve with roast potatoes and vegetables or with rice and salad.

Sri Lankan Chicken Curry

Ann Simon
Christchurch Council

Serves 4

60g (2 oz) vegetable ghee or 60ml (2 fl oz) of oil
2 medium onions, peeled and chopped
3 cloves of garlic, peeled and crushed
2.5 cm (1 in) piece of fresh root ginger, peeled and grated
½ teaspoon ground fenugreek
5 curry leaves
1 teaspoon turmeric
1 teaspoon hot chilli powder
1 teaspoon ground cumin
2 teaspoons ground coriander
2 tablespoons malt vinegar
1 teaspoon salt
1.4 kg (3 lb) thawed, or fresh chicken thighs
100g (3½ oz) chopped tomatoes (canned or fresh)
1 tablespoon tomato purée
1 teaspoon grated lemon rind
85g (3 oz) block of creamed coconut, chopped
15g (½ oz) fresh coriander leaves
600ml (1 pint) of water

Melt the ghee in large shallow saucepan or sauté pan with a lid. Add onions, garlic, ginger and fry until soft, stirring occasionally. Add fenugreek and curry leaves and fry for 1 minute. Then add in the remaining ground spices, vinegar and salt and fry for 5 minutes, stirring constantly.

Bone and cut the chicken into bite sized pieces. Add the chicken to the saucepan and cook until evenly browned and coated with the spice mixture. Stir in tomatoes, tomato purée and lemon rind and cook for 3 minutes.

Add the water and creamed coconut and stir until dissolved. Bring to the boil, reduce the heat, cover with the lid and simmer for 45 minutes - 1 hour.

Sprinkle with freshly chopped coriander leaves and serve with rice.

Steak and Ale Pie

Gary Webster
The Manor Arms, Burton

Serves 4

125ml (4 fl oz) olive oil
500g (1 lb) rib of beef or lean chuck steak, cubed
2 large onions, peeled and finely chopped
2 large carrots, peeled and finely chopped
2 leeks, washed and finely chopped
2 tablespoons tomato purée
120g (4 oz) plain flour
600ml (1 pint) dark bitter ale
600ml (1 pint) good brown veal (or beef) stock
600ml (1 pint) Guinness
Salt and freshly ground black pepper
500g (1 lb) ready made puff pastry
1 egg yolk beaten with 1 tablespoon water

Heat a heavy based large saucepan, carefully pour in the oil and when it begins to smoke add the steak. Allow it to seal and colour. Continue to cook the steak until the pan begins to become dry (i.e. the meat juices dry and begin to set as a glaze). Add the onions, carrots and leeks. Add the tomato purée and mix in well, leave to cook for 2 minutes stirring to prevent sticking. Add the flour, mix in well and cook on low heat for 10 minutes before stirring in the bitter ale, stock and Guinness. Simmer for 1¼ - 1½ hours until the meat is tender. Season to taste with salt and pepper. Leave to cool completely.

Place the filling into individual pie dishes or one large dish. If using individuals it is easiest to divide the pastry into 4 pieces. Roll out the pastry to approx. 5 mm (¼ in) thick and a little bigger than your dish. Cut a thin strip from around the edge. Damp the dish edge with water and cover with pastry strip. Damp this pastry. Roll the remaining pastry around your rolling pin, lift and unroll on to the dish. Trim off any excess pastry with a sharp knife and lightly press to seal the edges. "Knock up" the edges by pressing with your fingers on the top using a small sharp knife to tap at the cut side edge. With the knife point, cut a tiny hole in the centre of the top of allow steam to escape. Decorate with excess pastry if you wish, e.g. leaf shapes. Chill in the refrigerator 10 - 15 minutes while you pre-heat the oven to 220°C/425°F/Gas 7.

Brush the top, but not cut edges of the pastry, with the egg yolk mixture. Place the dish on a baking tray and bake 25 - 30 minutes until well risen and golden brown. Serve hot.

Bobotie

Sue Van In

A favourite South African dish from one of our South African Residents

Serves 6

> 1 kg (2 lb) minced lamb
> 1 thick slice white bread
> 250ml (8 fl oz) milk
> 2 tablespoons cooking oil
> 2 onions, finely chopped
> 3 teaspoons curry powder
> 1 tablespoon apricot jam
> 1 egg, beaten (optional)
> Raisins to taste
> 2 tablespoons lemon juice
> 6 lemon leaves

Topping

> 3 eggs
> 350ml (12 fl oz) milk
> Salt and pepper to taste

Pre-heat the oven to 160°C/315°F/Gas 2 - 3.
Grease a 1.8 litre (3 pint) pie dish or oven-proof dish.

Soak the bread in the milk until soft, then mash it with a fork.

Using a frying or sauté pan heat the oil, add the onions and cook until soft and lightly coloured. Add the curry powder and apricot jam. Continue to fry lightly for 1 - 2 minutes. Remove from the hob and add the minced lamb stirring the mixture with a fork until it is well distributed and lightly cooked. Add all the remaining ingredients except the lemon leaves and stir in well to combine. Spoon the meat mixture into the prepared dish and arrange the lemon leaves on top. Bake in the oven for 15 minutes.

Meanwhile prepare the topping, beat the eggs in a medium bowl, add the milk and season to taste. Pour the egg mixture over the bobotie and return the dish to the oven for a further 15 minutes.

Serve with yellow rice.

Ossoboco Milanese

Antonio Maggio Carluccio
Pinocchios Restaurant, Christchurch

Serves 4

4 veal marrow bones, 3-4 cm thick, cut from the middle shin
1 small onion, sliced
800g (1¾ lb) can Italian peeled tomatoes
Juice of 1 large orange
Grated rind of half a large orange
125ml (4 fl oz) dry red wine
Flour for dusting
Salt and freshly ground black pepper
4 tablespoons olive oil

Dust the marrow bones with the salt and flour. Heat the oil in a large casserole and fry the marrow bones on both sides, taking care not to damage the marrow in the centre or allow it to fall out. Remove the bones and put to one side.

Fry the onion in the casserole until transparent, add the tomatoes, plus half their juice, breaking them up with a wooden spoon while cooking. Keep the heat high so that the tomatoes reduce. After 5 minutes, add the grated orange rind, the orange juice and the red wine. Continue to cook over a high heat and return the marrow bones to the sauce.

Season with salt and pepper, reduce the heat, cover and simmer for 1 - 1½ hours or until the meat starts to come away from the bone.

Serve with rice.

Chicken Florentine Lasagne

Zoë Martin

Serves 4 - 6

2 tablespoons butter
2 tablespoons olive oil
1 onion, finely chopped
400g (14 oz) tin of tomatoes
2 x 400g (14 oz) tins of chicken in white sauce
60-90g (2-3 oz) mushrooms, thinly sliced
60-90g (2-3 oz) spinach
6 Slices Proscuitto
8 Sheets of Lasagne
Jar of Lasagne White Sauce (Béchamel Sauce)
Parmesan Cheese

Pre-heat the oven to 180°C/350°F/Gas 4.

Grease a shallow oven-proof dish with half of the butter.

Heat the oil and the rest of the butter in a medium sized saucepan and add the onion. Fry until soft and translucent (not browned) for a few minutes then add the tin of tomatoes and continue cooking until slightly reduced. Add the tins of chicken and heat through, mixing well. Leave to cool.

To prepare the spinach, place the leaves in a colander and pour over boiling water. Leave for a few moments and press out the excess water.

When the above are sufficiently cool assemble the dish. Spread **half** the chicken mixture on the base of the dish, then top with half the sliced mushrooms, spinach and three slices of proscuitto. Season with salt and pepper. Cover with sheets of lasagne. Repeat the layers.

Cover the top layer of lasagne with white sauce and sprinkle generously with Parmesan.

Bake in the oven for 35 - 40 minutes until golden brown and bubbling.

Finnish Meatballs

Hely Little

Serves 4 - 6

900g (2 lb) beef mince
1 large onion, chopped
1 egg, beaten
Garlic or curry powder (to taste)
Oil or butter for frying
Flour for coating
Salt and freshly ground pepper

Sauce

1 tin Oxtail or Mulligatawny soup
1 tin tomatoes

Pre-heat the oven to 150°C/300°F/Gas 2.

Place all the mince, onion, egg and seasonings in a bowl and mix well until the mixture is firm.

With your hands, roll the mixture into balls (about a golf ball size) and toss in the flour to lightly dust.

Fry the balls in the oil or butter until they are browned.

Place the soup, tomatoes and the prepared meatballs into a covered oven-proof dish and put in the oven for 1 - 1½ hours, stirring occasionally during the cooking process.

Best served with boiled or mashed potatoes and green vegetables.

HYVÄÄ RUAKA HALUA

TOIVOO HELY

Dorset Porkies

Paul & Rob
Ye Olde George, Christchurch

Serves 4

450g (1 lb) sausage meat
1 medium onion, finely chopped
1 medium cooking apple, peeled and finely chopped
1 teaspoon dry mixed herbs
Flour for coating
Salt and freshly ground pepper

Sauce

250ml (8 fl oz) orange juice
125ml (4 fl oz) pineapple juice
1 pepper, de-seeded and chopped
115g (4 oz) pineapple chunks
A splash of white wine vinegar
1 teaspoon arrowroot

Batter

115g (4 oz) plain flour
125ml (5 fl oz) water or lager
½ teaspoon salt

Mix the sausage meat, onion, apple and mixed herbs together, seasoning well. Divide the mixture into 16 and roll each piece into a sausage shape about 2 cm (1 in) thick. Coat each with the flour.

Mix the batter ingredients together. Coat each 'porkie' in the batter and deep fry for about 7 minutes until the sausage meat is thoroughly cooked. Remove and drain and keep warm.

Dissolve the arrowroot in a little water. Meanwhile place the remaining sauce ingredients in a saucepan over a medium heat and bring to the boil. Add the arrowroot, stirring continuously. Simmer until the sauce has thickened and reduced by about a half.

To serve, place 2 'porkies' on each plate and pour over the sweet and sour sauce. Serve with rice or chips and peas.

Beef and "49er" Casserole

Paul & Rob
Ye Olde George, Christchurch

Serves 8

1.8 kg (4 lb) braising steak, cut into cubes
2 large onions, chopped
1 clove garlic, crushed
Oil and butter for frying
Salt and freshly ground pepper
600ml (1 pint) Ringwood "49er" Bitter
1 beef stock cube.

Pre-heat the oven to 180°C/350°F/Gas 4.

Heat the oil and butter in a large casserole and seal the beef cubes (this is best achieved in batches).

Remove the beef from the casserole and set aside, add the onions and garlic and fry until translucent. Return the cooked beef to the casserole and add the beer and crumbled stock cube. Stir well.

Place in the oven for 1½ - 2 hours. Add extra stock/beer if necessary during cooking process.

Venison Casserole

A traditional recipe

Serves 4 - 6

> 1 kg (2 lb) venison, cubed
> 2 tablespoons cooking oil
> 2 onions, finely chopped
> Flour to coat
> 450ml (15 fl oz) stock (or beer/stout)
> 150ml (5 fl oz) port (or red wine)
> 175g (6 oz) field mushrooms, sliced
> 1 teaspoon juniper berries, crushed (optional)

Preheat the oven to 160°C/315°F/Gas 2 - 3.

Coat the venison cubes in seasoned flour, and in a large frying pan, heat half the oil and brown the meat in batches. Transfer the meat to a large casserole.

Heat the remaining oil in the frying pan and fry the onions until translucent, de-glaze the pan with some of the stock and add to the meat. Pour the remainder of the stock on the meat and add the crushed juniper berries, place in the oven covered for about 2 hours.

After 1 hours cooking, add the mushrooms and the port.

Serve with boiled leeks and mashed swede.

(Alternatively, 30 minutes before the end of the cooking time place slices of cooked potato over the top of the meat and brush with melted butter, replace in the oven uncovered.)

Baked Gammon with Mushrooms and Tomatoes

Jane Martin

Serves 4

750g (1¾ lb) gammon joint
115g (4 oz) mushrooms
4 medium sized tomatoes
85g (3 oz) soft brown sugar
2 teaspoons dry English mustard
60g (2 oz) butter, melted
2 tablespoons dry cider or apple juice

Pre-heat the oven to 190°C/375°F/Gas 5.

Put the gammon in a roasting dish. Cover with foil and bake in the oven for 1 hour.

In a non-metallic bowl, mix the sugar, mustard and butter. Add the cider and mix well.

Remove the dish from the oven and coat the gammon with the mixture. Halve the mushrooms and tomatoes and add to the roasting tin around the gammon. Return to the oven uncovered and continue cooking for another 20 minutes.

Remove the gammon, tomatoes and mushrooms from the roasting dish and keep warm.

Place the roasting dish on the hob and heat the juices remaining in the pan allowing to thicken slightly to produce a sauce.

Best served with whole or mashed potatoes and peas.

Fillet Steak Marinated in Tamarind Juice, Lemon Grass and Soy on a Bed of Coriander Scented Noodles

The Boathouse
Quomps, Christchurch

Serves 1

1 x 225g (8 oz) fillet steak
1 tablespoon tamarind juice
1 teaspoon dark soy sauce
1 stalk of lemon grass, finely chopped
1 bunch of fresh coriander
Dried egg noodles (approximately one "ball" per person)
1 teaspoon toasted sesame oil

In a non-metallic bowl, blend the tamarind juice with soy sauce and add the lemon grass. Prick the fillet steak with a knife and add to the marinade for at least 4 hours.

Put some water in a large saucepan and bring to the boil. Add the egg noodles and remove the pan from the heat and allow to stand covered for 5 - 8 minutes, stirring occasionally.

Remove the steak from the marinade and pat dry, grill for 8 - 10 minutes turning occasionally for a medium steak.

Chop the coriander, drain the noodles. Put the sesame oil in a hot wok and add the coriander and noodles, stir and allow the noodles to warm through.

Serve the steak on the noodles in a deep plate.

Pork Satay

Debbie Edlund

Serves 4 - 6

350g (12 oz) pork fillet, cubed
3 tablespoons cooking oil
1 tablespoon dark soy sauce
3 teaspoons ground cumin
1 onion, finely chopped
½ teaspoon chilli powder
1 teaspoon medium Madras curry powder
175g (6 oz) crunchy peanut butter
1 tablespoon honey
1 tablespoon tomato purée

In a non-metallic bowl, blend the 2 tablespoons of the oil with soy sauce and 1 teaspoon of the cumin. Add the pork cubes and marinade for 1 - 2 hours.

In a pan, add the remaining oil and fry the onion, add the chilli powder and curry powder and the remaining cumin and cook until the onion is softened. Add all the other ingredients with 200 ml (7 fl oz) water. Cook gently for 5 minutes.

Thread the pork onto skewers (if using bamboo skewers soak in water for 15 minutes first) and grill, turning frequently and brushing with the satay sauce, until the pork is cooked and browned.

Serve with the remaining satay sauce and rice.

Beef Medallions with Stilton Sauce

Mary Reader
Reader Communications

Serves 2

2 x 115g (4 oz) fillet steaks
1 teaspoon Dijon mustard
Salt and pepper
1 tablespoon oil
25g (¾ oz) butter
1 tablespoon brandy
1 tablespoon finely chopped shallots
A dash of Worcestershire sauce
50ml (1¾ fl oz) dry white wine
60g (2 oz) Stilton cheese, crumbled
100ml (3½ fl oz) double cream
A little fresh parsley, chopped

Rub the steaks with Dijon mustard and pepper. Heat a strong pan, add the oil, heat and add half the butter, then quickly brown the meat all over cooking for 2 - 4 minutes each side depending on how well done you like your steaks. Stir in the brandy. Remove the meat and keep warm.

Add the remaining butter to the pan then the shallots and stir-fry for fifteen seconds. Add the Worcestershire sauce and the wine and allow to bubble until reduced by half.

Add the Stilton and the cream, stir well to blend and return the steaks to the pan to heat through thoroughly. Sprinkle with chopped parsley and serve with a julienne of carrots and French beans.

Chicken and Bacon Risotto

Jane Martin

Serves 4

1 onion, finely chopped
2 tablespoons olive oil
30g (1 oz) butter
175g (6 oz) bacon, chopped
225g (8 oz) arborio rice
225g (8 oz) cooked chicken, cut into pieces
1 litre (1¾ pint) chicken stock
Salt and freshly ground black pepper
Parmesan cheese, to garnish

In a large heavy-based saucepan gently fry the onion in the oil and butter for about 2 minutes. Add the bacon and fry for another 3 minutes until the onion is soft but not coloured. Add the rice and stir for a further 2 minutes ensuring that all the rice is coated in the cooking oils. Add the cooked chicken and about ¼ of the chicken stock, stirring well. There will be a great deal of steam. Season to taste.

Add the remaining stock gradually in stages, allowing the rice to absorb the stock before adding more. The whole process should take about 20 - 30 minutes; the finished risotto should be creamy in texture while the rice is "al-dente".

Sprinkle with Parmesan cheese and serve immediately.

Note: Since this dish is made with cooked meat, it should not be re-heated.

Vegetarian Dishes & Vegetables

Throughout the centuries people who lived in Christchurch would have grown their own vegetables to eat and bought any that they could not provide for themselves in the market.

Root vegetables such as onions, garlic, leeks and cabbage have been mainstays of our cooking because their strong flavour masked the salty taste of preserved meat. Similarly these vegetables, along with peas and beans, could be dried or pickled for use when no fresh vegetables were available.

Edible mushrooms abound in the area and have always been used in cooking. Plants such as sea kale, growing wild on the cliff tops, and watercress found in the chalk rivers and streams would have provided additional free vegetables. Wild herbs would have been added to soups and broths and their leaves used in salads.

In the past vegetables would also have been used for medicinal purposes. For example, cabbage leaves made a suitable compress for swollen or painful joints and water in which an onion had been infused would have given relief to a colicky child.

J.Pain & Co Market Garden, Stour Road 1913

Alsace Onion Tart

Ian Naughton, Sous Chef
Pommery's, Christchurch

Serves 6

400g (14 oz) plain flour, sieved
A pinch of salt
200g (7 oz) lightly salted butter, diced, at room temperature
Approximately 4 tablespoons water

Filling

6 large onions, finely chopped
1 clove garlic, peeled then crushed with salt
30g (1 oz) lightly salted butter
Salt and black pepper
A pinch of fresh thyme leaves
560ml (18 fl oz) whipping cream
5 eggs, beaten

Put flour, salt and butter into a blender and process until the mixture resembles breadcrumbs. Add the water and continue blending until the mixture comes together and forms a dough. Wrap in cling film and chill for 20 minutes.

Have ready a 23 - 25 cm (9 - 10 in) deep flan ring on a baking tray or, a flan tin with a removable base. Line the flan ring with the pastry and chill while pre-heating the oven to 180°C /350°F/Gas 4. Bake blind for 15 minutes and remove from the oven.

Reduce the oven temperature to 150°C/300°F/Gas 2.

To make the filling: In a large pan over a low heat slowly sweat the onion and garlic in the butter until soft and transparent. Season with salt and pepper. Add the thyme. Stir in the cream, bring almost to boiling point and remove from the heat. Pour the warm mixture on to the eggs and quickly stir together. Put the mixture into the pastry case and bake for a further 30 minutes until set and lightly golden.

Ideal to serve with rocket or salad leaves tossed lightly with balsamic vinegar and olive oil.

Voracious Vegetable Bake

Delia Allen

Serves 6

1 tablespoon olive oil
2 carrots, diced
2 red onions, diced
4 celery sticks, diced
225g (8 oz) mushrooms, sliced
1 green pepper, sliced
½ red pepper, sliced
½ yellow pepper, sliced
1 clove garlic, crushed or finely chopped
400g (14 oz) can chopped tomatoes
1 teaspoon tomato purée
400g (14 oz) can kidney beans
115g (4 oz) wholemeal breadcrumbs
3 teaspoons sesame seeds
100g (3½ oz) Cheddar cheese, grated

Have ready a 1.7 litre (2 pint) capacity shallow oven-proof dish. Heat the oil in a large saucepan. Add the carrots, onions, celery, mushrooms, peppers and garlic. Stir to mix, lower the heat, then cover and cook until tender, for about 15 minutes.

Stir in the tomatoes, tomato purée and kidney beans, and season to taste with salt and pepper. Simmer gently for about 18 minutes, stirring occasionally, then remove from the heat. Pre-heat the oven to 180°C/350°F/Gas 4.

Using a small bowl mix the breadcrumbs, sesame seeds and cheese together. Stir half of this mixture into the cooked vegetables and put the remaining half to one side. Spoon the vegetable mixture into the oven-proof dish and sprinkle with the remaining half of the breadcrumb mixture to cover. Bake in the oven for about 20 minutes or until golden.

Note: The flavour of the bake can be altered by using other vegetables such as parsnips, courgettes, leeks, aubergines or shallots either as substitutes or in addition. Experiment until you discover your favourite mixture.

Potato Gateaux

Lyn Taylor

Serves 8

1.1 kg (2¼ lb) peeled potatoes
15g (½ oz) butter
115g (4 oz) breadcrumbs, toasted and fried in 30g (1 oz) butter
150ml (5 fl oz) single cream
2 eggs separated
1 clove garlic, peeled and crushed
115g (4 oz) diced cheddar cheese
Salt and pepper
A few small sprigs parsley

Put the potatoes into lightly salted water, bring to the boil, then simmer until tender. Meanwhile prepare an 18 cm (7 in) cake tin. Thickly smear the base and sides of the tin with the 15g (½ oz) of butter. Press the crispy breadcrumbs over the base and sides reserving enough to sprinkle on top later.

Pre-heat the oven to 200°C/400°F/Gas 6.

Drain the potatoes, mash until smooth, then beat in the cream, the egg yolks, garlic and salt and pepper. Fold in the cheese. Whisk the egg whites to stiff and fold them into the mixture.

Place the mixture into the prepared tin, smooth over, then sprinkle with the remaining crumbs.

Bake in the oven for 20 minutes. Turn out on to a serving dish and garnish with parsley.

Vegetable Quiche

Ian Morton, Head Chef
The Avonmouth Hotel

Serves 6 – 8

Pastry

175g (6 oz) plain flour
85g (3 oz) butter, chilled
85g (3 oz) cheese, grated, e.g. Gruyère or Cheddar
Water to mix

Filling

2 tablespoons oil
1 medium onion chopped
1 x 400g (14 oz) can tomatoes, drain, chop and drain again
1 clove garlic, peeled and crushed
½ teaspoon dried basil
225g (8 oz) broccoli, in large florets, blanched and drained
85g (3 oz) Gruyère cheese, grated
3 medium eggs, beaten
200ml (7 fl oz) whipping cream
Salt, pepper and a pinch of ground nutmeg

Have ready a 25 cm (10 in) flan ring set on a baking tray or a flan tin.

To make the pastry: In a medium sized bowl rub the butter into the flour, toss in the cheese and add water to mix. Knead lightly until smooth, wrap in cling film and chill for 20 minutes. Roll out the pastry to a circle sufficiently large to line the flan ring and chill the pastry lined flan while pre-heating the oven to 180°C/350°F/Gas 4.

Bake the pastry blind for about 20 minutes till firm. Remove the blind filling and bake a further 5 minutes.

Meanwhile, heat the oil and fry the onion slowly till soft. Add the tomatoes and fry quickly to lightly soften. Add the garlic, basil and nutmeg and fry for 1 minute. Remove from the heat and season with salt and pepper. Evenly disperse the tomato mixture and broccoli into the pastry. Sprinkle with the Gruyère cheese.

Whisk the eggs and cream together, and gently pour over the vegetables. Return to the oven for 20 - 30 minutes to bake until set and golden brown.

Vegetable Chow Mein
(Stir fry noodles with mange tout, bean sprouts and carrots)

Francesca Tse

Serves 4

280g (10 oz) egg noodles
2 tablespoons sunflower oil
1 small onion, sliced
1 large carrot, shredded thinly
175g (6 oz) mange tout, trimmed and halved
115g (4 oz) bean sprouts
1 spring onion, sliced diagonally
2 tablespoons light soy sauce
1 teaspoon salt
1 tablespoon sweet sherry

Bring a large pan of lightly salted water to the boil. Add the noodles and cook for 5 minutes. Drain and reserve.

Heat the oil in a large frying pan or wok. Add the onions and stir fry for 3 minutes. Add the carrots, mange tout and bean sprouts. Stir fry for 2 minutes.

Add the noodles, spring onions and soy sauce. Season to taste and stir fry until piping hot. STIR FREQUENTLY. Then add the sweet sherry.

Serve immediately.

Note: Always cut the vegetables into very thin strips so that they cook quickly to retain their full flavour and crispness.

Spinach Frittata

Susan Eckstein

A quick and easy dish to serve as light main course.

Serves 6 as a starter, 4 as a main course

1½ tablespoons olive oil
1 small onion thinly sliced
375g (13 oz) frozen leaf spinach, thawed and drained well
6 large eggs
25g (¾ oz) freshly grated Parmesan cheese
1 tablespoon chopped or finely shredded basil leaves

In a large frying pan heat the oil, add the onion and fry on a low heat until soft. Stir in the spinach and cook for 2 - 3 minutes to dry off any excess moisture, remove from the hob.

In a large bowl beat the eggs with the cheese, season well and stir in the spinach mixture and the basil.

Pour back into the frying pan and ensure the spinach is evenly distributed. Cook on low to medium heat until the egg is set. The surface may be a little soft so slide the pan under a hot grill to set it.

To serve, cut into wedges and serve either warm or cool at room temperature. A crispy salad and ciabatta or focaccia breads are perfect accompaniments. A salsa or chutney gives extra zing!

Variation: In place of the spinach use sliced courgettes and cook with the onion to soften. Use marjoram or parsley instead of the basil.

Vegetarian Nut Loaf

Mike Duvall
The Copper Skillet

Half a large wholemeal loaf
2 large onions, sliced
2 cloves garlic, peeled and crushed
200g (7 oz) mushrooms, sliced
Oregano
Worcestershire sauce
145g (5 oz) mature Cheddar cheese
200g (7 oz) broken walnuts
3 eggs
Salt and pepper

Crumb the bread into a large mixing bowl.

Sweat the onion and garlic until soft, adding the mushrooms during the cooking. Remove from the heat and add to the bread. Season with salt and pepper, a sprinkling of oregano and about five dashes of Worcestershire sauce. Then add the cheese, walnuts and eggs. Mix together thoroughly.

Line a loaf tin with oiled greaseproof paper and pour in the mixture.

Cook in a low oven 140°C/275°F/Gas 1 for 1½ hours.

Allow to cool in the tin, then turn out.
(If this proves difficult, heat the base of the tin slightly)

The loaf can be served with a variety of accompaniments, mushroom gravy has proved very popular.

Vegetable Casserole

Josephine Spencer

Serves 4

40g (1½ oz) butter or margarine
1 large onion, sliced
600ml (1 pint) vegetable stock
1 tablespoon tomato purée
1 teaspoon mixed herbs
2 large carrots, sliced
2 leeks, sliced
1 large parsnip, sliced
675g (1½ lb) potatoes, sliced
85g (3 oz) grated cheese
Salt and freshly milled black pepper

Heat the oven to 180°C/350°F/Gas 4.

Melt half the fat in a saucepan. Add the onion and fry until golden. Remove from the heat.

Stir in the stock, tomato purée, herbs and seasoning. Add the carrots, leeks, parsnip and one third of the potatoes. Mix well then turn the mixture into a casserole. Arrange the remaining potato slices over the top and dot with the remaining butter/margarine.

Cover and bake in the oven for 50 minutes.

At the end of this cooking time, increase the oven temperature to 220°C/425°F/Gas 7, remove the cover and sprinkle the cheese over, then cook the casserole uncovered for a further 20 minutes.

Perfect Chips

Paul Leccacorvi
Captain Cod

450g (1 lb) Maris Piper potatoes
Oil for frying
Sea salt

Peel and cut the potatoes into approx. 1 cm (½ in) chips.

Rinse the chips in cold water to remove all the starch.

Dry the chips thoroughly on a tea towel or kitchen paper.
(It is crucial that the chips must be dry before being cooked.)

In a deep fat fryer, heat the oil to 150°C (300°F), slowly place a handful of chips in the oil and cook until just soft, but not coloured. Remove the chips from the oil and allow to cool completely. Repeat the process until all the chips have been cooked.

Re-heat the oil to 180°C (350°F). Place all the chips back into the oil and cook until golden.

Drain and sprinkle with sea salt.

Sweet Potato and Okra Strudel
with Spring Onion Salsa

Claudio Esperanca
The Boathouse, Christchurch

Serves 2

1 sweet potato, diced
1 clove of garlic, chopped
1 teaspoon ground cumin
1 teaspoon caraway seeds
1 stick of cinnamon
200g (7 oz) okra
Salt and pepper
Juice of 1 lemon
1 bunch of coriander
½ red chilli
1 packet puff pastry
Salt and pepper
Olive oil for frying

Salsa

1 bunch of spring onions
½ onion, grated
1 tablespoon vinegar
1 tablespoon sugar

Heat olive oil in a pan and add half the coriander, half the garlic and the cumin and caraway seed. Cook for 5 minutes, stirring occasionally. Add the sweet potato and allow to brown. Cover with boiling water and cook the potato until soft adding more liquid if necessary.

Drain and allow to cool.

Dice the okra, and put into a colander and sprinkle with the lemon juice. Allow to drain for 5 minutes.

In another saucepan, heat some olive oil. Add the remaining coriander, garlic and red chilli. Add the okra. Cook for about 10 minutes on a low heat until it is tender. Drain and allow to cool.

Roll out a square with the thawed puff pastry of side 10 cm (4 in). Mix the cool sweet potato and okra together and fill the pastry square with the mixture, rolling into the shape of an envelope. Brush with egg wash and bake in the oven until golden brown.

To prepare the salsa, wash and dice the spring onion. Mix it with the onion, vinegar and sugar.

To serve, cut across the parcel diagonally and serve garnished with plenty of salsa.

White Cabbage with Caraway Seeds

The Boathouse
Quomps, Christchurch

1 kg (2¼ lb) white cabbage, shredded
1½ teaspoons caraway seeds
1 clove of garlic, chopped
½ white onion, grated
2 tablespoons olive oil
Salt & freshly ground pepper

In a saucepan, fry the onion and garlic in the olive oil for 3 - 4 minutes until softened. Add the caraway seeds and continue to cook for 3 minutes more. Add the shredded cabbage and cook for a further 5 minutes, then add sufficient boiling water, about a small cup, to just moisten the cabbage. Cover, reduce the heat to low and cook for a further 5 minutes until the cabbage is tender.

Season with salt and pepper.

Carrot, Ginger & Orange Purée

The Boathouse
Quomps, Christchurch

1 clove of garlic, chopped
½ white onion, grated
1 teaspoon ginger, diced
1 kg (2¼ lb) carrots, sliced
1 teaspoon orange rind, grated
250ml (8 fl oz) orange juice
2 tablespoons olive oil
Salt & freshly ground pepper

In a saucepan, fry the onion and garlic in the olive oil for 2 - 3 minutes until softened. Add the ginger and continue to cook for 2 minutes more. Add the sliced carrots and orange rind and cook for a further 10 minutes, add the orange juice and continue to cook until the carrots are tender, adding boiling water if necessary. When the carrots are soft, season with salt and pepper and blend the carrots with the cooking liquid in a food processor until a creamy consistency.

French Beans with Shallots
And White Wine

225g (8 oz) shallots, peeled and finely diced
2 tablespoons olive oil
125ml (4 fl oz) white wine
1 kg (2¼ lb) French beans, trimmed

Sauté the shallots in the olive oil for 3 - 4 minutes, add the white wine and allow to reduce.

Add the French beans and cook for 8 - 10 minutes until "al-dente".

Hot Spicy Potato Wedges

Elizabeth Richardson

1.2 kg (2 lb) large potatoes
1 tablespoon of sunflower/olive oil
2 tablespoons wholemeal breadcrumbs
A large pinch of Cayenne pepper
1 teaspoon ground cumin
1 teaspoon garlic salt
1 teaspoon paprika
1 teaspoon ground black pepper
1 teaspoon mixed herbs

Pre-heat the oven to 220°C/425°F/Gas 7.

Scrub the potatoes leaving the skins on, then cut each one lengthways into eight wedges.

Place the wedges in a large mixing bowl add the oil and toss to coat the wedges evenly.

Mix together the breadcrumbs, Cayenne pepper, cumin, garlic salt, paprika, black pepper and herbs in another bowl. Then add to the potatoes and toss them again to evenly coat with the spice mixture.

Arrange the wedges in a single layer on a baking sheet and bake in the preheated oven for 35 - 40 minutes until they are golden brown and crisp.

Best served hot.

Greek Red Vegetable Bake

Anne Wilkinson
Christchurch Council

Serves 4

2 large aubergines, sliced into thick rounds
1 large red pepper, halved and seeded
Good quality olive oil for frying
1 large onion, peeled and chopped
2 large cloves garlic, peeled and chopped
1 teaspoon dried oregano
100ml (3½ fl oz) red wine
400g (14 oz) can chopped tomatoes
175g (6 oz) Greek black olives, halved and stoned
225g (8 oz) feta cheese
Ground black pepper

You will need a deep 1.5 – 1.8 litre (2½ - 3 pint) oven-proof casserole dish.

To prepare the vegetables: Put the aubergine slices into a colander, salting thoroughly through the layers. This draws out any bitter juice.

Leave to stand for 5 minutes, rinse and pat dry. Heat the grill to highest setting. Brush the aubergine with olive oil then grill for 2 - 3 minutes on each side. Now grill the pepper, without oil, skin side up until the skin blackens and blisters. To remove the skin; while it is still hot carefully put the pepper into a plastic bag and leave for 5 minutes. The skin will now be loose and easy to remove. Dice the flesh.

To make the tomato sauce: Heat a little olive oil in a sauté or covered frying pan. Cook the onions on a medium heat until just turning transparent. Add the garlic and oregano. Fry for 1 minute and add the wine, tomatoes and tomato purée. Season with pepper, turn the heat down to a slow simmer, cover and cook for 10 minutes. The sauce should be fairly thick. If not, uncover and cook for a few minutes more. Stir in the olives and red pepper.

Pre-heat the oven to 200°C/400°F/Gas 6.

To complete the dish: Layer the ingredients into the casserole dish starting with aubergine, tomato sauce and cheese. (If you keep the sauce layers fairly shallow the bake will be easier to lift out for serving). Finish with a good sprinkling of cheese and bake in the oven for 20 minutes, until the top is browned.

An appropriate accompaniment would be a salad and pitta bread, or plain boiled brown rice.

Note: In this recipe the best olives to use are the Greek black olives that have been in a brine then allowed to dry, hence their saltiness and wrinkly skins. They season the dish without the need of extra salt.

Sweets & Desserts

The 17th century was a great age of innovation in the cooking of sweets and puddings. One invention was the pudding cloth and this gave rise to a wide range of sweet steamed puddings. Other popular desserts such as bread and butter pudding, rice pudding and crème brûlée date from this time.

Plum puddings were favoured but for some reason they were banned during the Commonwealth period as they were considered unfit for God-fearing people!

Banquets or dinner parties during the 1700's were extravagant with many courses. A menu for a dinner of five courses is recorded as having for its last course 7 separate dishes: iced cream, raspberries, cherries, plums, apricots, gooseberries and currants served in glasses, almond cream and almond butter. The centre piece was a pyramid of sweetmeats and fruits. Dishes for the previous course included jellies and blancmanges, tarts, cheesecakes and custards as well as roast meat and fish dishes. Most courses did in fact provide a range of sweet and savoury foods.

Christchurch High Street, towards the Antelope Hotel

Chocolate and Ginger Cheesecake

James Martin

Serves 2

35g (1¼ oz) butter (at room temperature)
4 digestive biscuits, finely crushed
1 jar of ginger in syrup
3 tablespoons dark cocoa powder
Finely grated zest and juice of 1 orange
4 tablespoons double cream
2 tablespoons icing sugar
280g (10 oz) full fat mascarpone cheese
145g (5 oz) strawberries
Fresh mint sprigs to decorate

In a bowl, beat the butter until soft and creamy. Mix in the crushed biscuits and a little of the ginger syrup. Place the mixture in the base of two small rings.

Mix the cocoa powder with the orange juice and zest to a paste. Add the cream, icing sugar, 1 tablespoon diced ginger and the mascarpone cheese. Slowly and gently mix together. Pour into the rings on the crumb base and smooth the surface. Top with about 6 of the strawberries thinly sliced. Chill.

Cut the remaining ginger into thin strips.

To serve, place in the centre of the plates and remove the rings. Garnish around the base of each plate with the ginger strips and the rest of the syrup from the jar. Place the remaining strawberries, halved, around the plate and decorate with some sprigs of fresh mint.

Raspberry Tart

Patrick Anthony

Serves 4

3 large egg yolks
175ml (6 fl oz) double cream
50g (2 oz) granulated sugar
23-25 cm (9-10 in) pre-baked shortcrust pastry shell
225-275g (8-10 oz) fresh raspberries
2 tablespoons icing sugar

Pre-heat the oven to 190°C/375°F/Gas 5.

In a large bowl, beat the egg yolks with a fork. Pour in the cream and the granulated sugar and mix together until thoroughly blended.

Pour the mixture into the prepared pastry shell. Arrange the raspberries in a single layer all over the top of the mixture. Cook in the centre of the oven until the cream filling begins to set, about 20 - 30 minutes.

Leave to cool completely and sprinkle with the icing sugar before serving.

Fruit and Almond Tart

Patrick Anthony

Serves 4

145g (5 oz) ground almonds
1 large egg, lightly beaten
50-75g (2-3 oz) granulated sugar
2 tablespoons kirsch liqueur
175ml (6 fl oz) crème fraîche or double cream
450-560g (1-1¼ lb) sliced or diced fruit
(pears, peaches, cherries, plums or nectarines)
9-10 in (23-25 cm) pre-baked shortcrust pastry shell
1 tablespoon caster sugar

Pre-heat the oven to 190°C/375°F/Gas 5.

In a large bowl, thoroughly blend together the almonds, egg, granulated sugar, kirsch and crème fraîche, until quite smooth.

Arrange the prepared fruit in the pastry shell. Carefully pour the cream filling all over the top. Cook in the centre of the oven until the cream filling has set, about 45 minutes.

Remove from the oven and sprinkle with the caster sugar.

Serve the tart warm or at room temperature with cream or ice-cream.

Pear Filled with
Chocolate & Amaretto Sabayon

Anton Edelmann
Maître Chef des Cuisines
The Savoy Hotel, London

Serves 4

1 litre (1¾ pints) water
500g (1 lb) caster sugar
1 cinnamon stick
4 dessert pears, ripe but firm
175g (6 oz) good quality dark chocolate (70% cocoa solids)
200g (7 oz) puff pastry
1 egg, beaten

Sabayon

5 egg yolks
75g (2½ oz) caster sugar
100ml (3½ fl oz) Amaretto

To make the stock syrup: In a medium pan gently heat the water, caster sugar and cinnamon stick, stirring frequently to dissolve the sugar. Bring the syrup to the boil and cook at a fast bubble for 1 minute, then turn down the heat to a simmer.

Peel the pears and remove the core going in from the base with a Parisienne scoop (or a small melon baller) working as high as possible into the pear.

Place the pears into the stock syrup and poach for 2 minutes, then lift the pears out of the syrup and refresh them in cold water. Drain well.

Bring a medium pan of water to the boil. Remove from the heat. Put the chocolate into a bowl and place this over the pan to melt the chocolate, stirring occasionally (do not let the base of the bowl come into contact with the boiling water).

Place the pears, stalk down, into narrow tall cups and pour in the chocolate to fill them where the core was. Refrigerate until set.

Roll out the puff pastry to 2 mm ($^1/_8$ inch) thick and cut into 4 pieces. Place a pear in the centre of each and wrap it up. Brush the edges of the pastry with beaten egg and press on well to seal. Place on a baking tray, brush all over with beaten egg then chill in the refrigerator for 20 minutes.

Meanwhile pre-heat the oven to 190°C/375°F/Gas 5.

Bake the pears for approximately 20 minutes until golden brown and crisp.

To prepare the sabayon: Bring a medium pan, half full of water to the boil, then turn down to a simmer. Place the egg yolks, sugar and Amaretto in a bowl over, but not touching the water. Whisk to a light frothy mixture that will just hold its shape.

To serve, place each pear in the middle of a plate and pour the warm sabayon around.

Millefeuille of Winter Fruits
with Champagne Syllabub

James Penn, Head Chef
Waterford Lodge Hotel

Serves 4

225g (8 oz) good quality puff pastry
2 clementines, peeled and segmented
1 pear, peeled if wished, quartered, cored, sliced
4 figs, sliced
2 russet apples, quartered, cored, sliced
300ml (10 fl oz) double cream
1 teaspoon caster sugar
2-3 drops of vanilla essence

Syllabub

Finely grated zest of 1 lemon
½ glass champagne
115g (4 oz) caster sugar
300ml (10 fl oz) double cream

Icing sugar
A little fresh mint

Soak the lemon zest in the champagne for a minimum of 5 hours.

Roll out the pastry to a square 1 cm (½ in) thick. Trim to neaten the edges and cut into 4 squares. Place on a lightly greased and dampened baking tray. Score the top of the pastry to a pattern of your choice.

Chill in the refrigerator while pre-heating the oven to 220°C/425°F/Gas 7.

Bake the pastry for 25 - 30 minutes until well risen, crisp and golden. Remove from the baking tray and cool on a wire rack.

Whisk the cream with the teaspoon of caster sugar, and vanilla essence to taste.
Slice each pastry horizontally into 3 layers.

To assemble, arrange the cream and fruits on the base and middle layers. Replace the scored top piece. Chill while making the syllabub.

To make the syllabub, using a large bowl stir the sugar into the lemon zest and champagne mixture until dissolved. Slowly add the cream and whisk until soft peaks form as the whisk is lifted away.

To serve, pour syllabub on to the centre of four plates. Place the millefeuille on top and dust with sifted sugar. Decorate with a sprig or leaves of fresh mint.

Blackberry Ice Cream

Ann Hyde
Bookends Bookshop

Makes approximately 2½ litres (4½ pints)

    1.4 kg (3 lb) blackberries
    450g (1 lb) icing sugar
    Juice of 1 lemon
    600ml (1 pint) double cream
    150ml (5 fl oz) water

Cook the blackberries in the water until soft and press through a sieve to extract all juice – hard work but worth it! Add the sugar and lemon juice to the blackberry juice. Lightly whip the cream. It should leave a trail when the whisk is lifted away, but just run when the bowl is tipped. Fold the cream into the blackberry juice. Pour into a container and freeze until slushy. Turn out and beat until creamy then freeze again.

Stunning!

Christmas Jelly Pudding

Vee Young

Serves 6

1 packet red jelly
175g (6 oz) dried mixed fruit
115g (4 oz) glacé cherries
60g (2 oz) crystallised ginger
115g (4 oz) canned pineapple, drained, keep the juice
60g (2 oz) mixed nuts, chopped
4 tablespoons sherry, rum or brandy
½ teaspoon cinnamon
½ teaspoon mixed spice
A large pinch of nutmeg

Cube the pineapple. Using a large bowl soak all the fruit in the pineapple juice overnight.

Make the jelly by stirring with 150 ml (5 fl oz) boiling water to melt and then leave to cool. Stir over well-iced water until the jelly begins to thicken. Immediately mix all the ingredients into the jelly. Pour into a 850 ml (1½ pint) Pyrex pudding bowl.

Chill in the refrigerator until set. Turn out on to a chilled plate and serve with cream.

Opposite: *Vegetable Chow Mein (see p.109)*
Next page: *Roasted Monkfish and Lobster with Roasted Garlic and Rosemary Jus (see p.64)*

Tiramisu

Rose Philpotts

Serves 4

1 packet sponge fingers
3 tablespoons Amaretto liqueur
3 tablespoons strong black coffee
3 eggs, separated
3 tablespoons caster sugar
225g (8 oz) Mascarpone cheese
Cocoa powder
Finely grated dark chocolate, optional

Mix the Amaretto and coffee together and then soak the sponge fingers in the mixture.

Have ready a 25 cm (10 in) x 5 cm (2 in) deep round dish. Use half of the sponge fingers to line the base of the dish.

Whisk the egg yolks and the sugar till pale and thick. Beat in the Mascarpone cheese being careful not to overwork the mixture. Whisk the egg whites until firm and just standing in peaks. Carefully fold the egg white into the cheese mixture.

Use half the mixture to cover the sponge fingers in the dish, sprinkle with sifted cocoa powder. Place the remaining soaked sponge fingers as a layer on top and cover these with the remaining cheese mixture, then smooth the surface. Chill for several hours.

To serve, sift over cocoa powder or sprinkle with grated chocolate to cover the surface evenly.

Previous page: *Steamed Lemon Puddings with Raspberry Sauce (see p.147)*
Opposite: *Tiramisu with Caramelised Oranges*

Fruit Crumble

Meg Bridgwater

Serves 4

675g (1½ lb) prepared fruit – raspberries/redcurrants
2 tablespoons of port (optional)
3 tablespoons of sugar to taste

Crumble Topping

175g (6 oz) plain flour
85g (3 oz) butter or margarine, diced
85g (3 oz) caster or demerara sugar
1 packet of amaretti biscuits, crushed to crumbs

Place the fruit in an oven proof dish, sprinkle with a little sugar if required, add the port.

Pre-heat the oven to 190°C/375°F/Gas 5.

If using a food processor, add flour, butter and sugar and process until the mixture resembles breadcrumbs, or if making by hand, rub the butter into the flour to resemble breadcrumbs then toss in the sugar to mix through evenly.

Sprinkle the crumble over the fruit then spread the amaretti crumbs evenly over the top.

Bake in the pre-heated oven until golden, approximately 30 - 40 minutes.

Serve with clotted cream or custard.

Other fruits may be used, e.g. fruits of the forest, apples, apricots, mandarin oranges, with Cointreau optional.

Amaretto Creams

Ian Morton, Head Chef
The Avonmouth Hotel, Mudeford

Serves 4 - 5

4 egg yolks
50g (1¾ oz) caster sugar
300ml (10 fl oz) full fat milk
1 tablespoon Amaretto liqueur
3 leaves gelatine, soaked 5 minutes in cold water to soften
300ml (10 fl oz) whipping or double cream.

Have ready 5 individual ramekins approximately 150 ml (¼ pint) capacity. In a medium sized bowl whisk the egg yolks and sugar, until pale and thick.

In a small saucepan heat the milk and Amaretto together, but do not boil. Pour the milk on to the egg yolk mixture, stir to blend and pour back into the pan. Over a low heat, stir continuously with a wooden spoon until the mixture coats the spoon. Do not allow it to boil.

Squeeze out the gelatine and stir it into the mixture until melted. Strain through a fine sieve into a clean pan or bowl and leave to cool. Meanwhile, whisk the cream until it leaves a good trail or very soft peaks when the whisk is lifted away.

Place the container of Amaretto mixture into a bowl of iced water. Stir continuously with a plastic spatula until the mixture begins to thicken. Quickly fold in the whipped cream, pour into the ramekins and chill until set.

Serve with a rich sweet almond biscuit.

Dark or White Chocolate Mousse

Ian Morton, Head Chef
The Avonmouth Hotel, Mudeford

Serves 8 - 10

> 3 eggs, separated
> 50g (1¾ oz) caster sugar
> 30g (1 oz) caster sugar
> 280g (10 oz) dark chocolate, chopped
> OR
> 425g (15 oz) white chocolate, chopped
> 225ml (7½ fl oz) whipping or double cream, lightly whipped.

<u>Praline</u>

> 115g (4 oz) caster sugar
> 1 tablespoon water
> 50g (1¾ oz) almonds, toasted
> 50g (1¾ oz) hazelnuts, toasted

Bring a pan of water to the boil, remove from the heat. Place a bowl containing the chocolate over the water. Stir occasionally to melt the chocolate, remove the bowl and allow to cool to room temperature without setting.

Re-boil the water, remove from the heat. Using another bowl put in the egg yolks and the 50g (1¾ oz) caster sugar. Place over the water. Whisk until pale and thick, remove the bowl and whisk until cool.

Now whisk the egg whites, add the remaining 30g (1 oz) caster sugar and whisk to hold stiff peaks. Fold the egg white into the yolk mixture. Fold the chocolate into the cream and then fold the chocolate and egg mixtures together. Pour into the ramekins and leave to set in the refrigerator.

To serve, remove from the refrigerator and sprinkle with praline if you want to give an extra special finish.

To make the praline: Prepare a baking tray lined with non-stick baking parchment. Place the sugar and water into a small heavy based pan. Heat gently to melt the sugar then bubble to caramel. Stir in the nuts and pour the mixture on to the prepared tray. Leave to cool.

DO NOT TOUCH AT ANY TIME UNTIL COOL AND SET. HOT SUGAR WILL GIVE A SEVERE BURN.

Crack and remove from the paper. Grind in a food processor or blender. (Sieve if you prefer a finer finish, but a crunch goes well with the smooth mousse).

Terrine of Fruits

Ian Morton, Head Chef
The Avonmouth Hotel, Mudeford

Serves 8

10 gelatine leaves, soaked for 5 minutes in cold water
450ml (16 fl oz) orange juice
115g (4 oz) caster sugar
1 tablespoon Cointreau
675g (1½ lb) soft fruits of your choice

Have ready a terrine or loaf shaped mould approximately 1½ litre (2½ lb) loaf tin.

Using a medium sized pan bring the orange juice and sugar just to the boil. Skim and remove from the heat. Lightly squeeze out the gelatine and add it to the orange juice with the Cointreau. Stir for 30 seconds to melt the gelatine then strain through a fine sieve. Pour a small layer into the terrine mould, chill until set.

Prepare the chosen fruit as necessary, e.g. whole berries, segments of citrus fruits, slices of peach, etc and place in the terrine to come level with the top. Pour the remaining orange jelly over the fruits and chill for twelve hours until set.

To serve, turn out and slice. A neat spoonful of whipped cream may be placed on or next to the slice.

Amanda's Amazing Cheesecake

Amanda Bradshaw

Serves 6 - 8

145g (5 oz) digestive biscuit crumbs
2 tablespoons granulated sugar
115g (4 oz) butter, melted
115g (4 oz) cream cheese
115g (4 oz) icing sugar
300ml (10 fl oz) double cream
350g (12 oz) can of fruit pie filling e.g. cherry or apricot

Have ready a 20 cm (8 in) round, loose-bottomed cake tin.
Pre-heat the oven to 180°C/350°F/Gas 4.

Place the biscuit crumbs and granulated sugar in a bowl. Pour in the butter and stir until well mixed. Press the mixture into the base of the tin. Bake in the oven for 5 minutes. Remove from the oven and leave to cool completely.

Using a medium sized bowl beat the cream cheese and icing sugar together until smooth and creamy. Whisk the cream until stiff enough to hold light peaks as the whisk is lifted away. Fold the two mixtures together until combined. Spoon on to the cold biscuit base and smooth the top. Finally, top with the fruit pie filling and chill well in the refrigerator to set.

Chocolate Pudding Soufflé

Neal Heyworth
Splinters, Christchurch

A favourite recipe of the pastry Chef at Splinters, Neal Heyworth.
A delicious dessert which is very easy to prepare and will go down a treat at any dinner party.

Serves 4

100g (3½ oz) good quality dark cooking chocolate
100g (3½ oz) lightly salted butter
Finely grated zest of 1 orange
2 large eggs plus 2 large yolks
50g (1¾ oz) caster sugar
35g (1¼ oz) plain flour
A little melted butter, to prepare dishes
A little extra flour, to prepare dishes

Pre-heat the oven to 190°C/375°F/Gas 5.

Lightly grease four ramekins approximately 150 ml (¼ pint) capacity each with melted butter. Place a disc of non-stick baking paper in each base and brush again with melted butter. Dust with flour, emptying out any excess. Place them on a baking tray.

Place a pan half full of water on the hob, bring to the boil, reduce the heat to barely a simmer.

Put the chocolate, butter and orange zest into a bowl to fit over the pan without touching the water. Place the bowl over the water. Stir occasionally until the chocolate and butter have melted and the mixture is smooth. Remove the bowl and leave to cool thoroughly while preparing the egg mixture.

In a separate bowl, whisk together the eggs, egg yolks and sugar until thick and pale and the mixture leaves a trail when the whisk is lifted away. Carefully fold the egg mixture into the chocolate and butter. Finally, gently fold in the flour until it is dispersed throughout the mixture. Divide evenly into the prepared ramekins and bake in the oven for 8 minutes.

After baking each "Soufflé" can be turned out of the ramekin and served on a dessert plate with either double or clotted cream. The centre of the Chocolate Pudding Soufflé will still "ooze" with chocolate.

Malva Pudding

Joanne Woodifield

Serves 6

1 large egg
1 cup caster sugar
1 tablespoon smooth apricot jam
1 cup plain flour
1 teaspoon bicarbonate of soda
A generous pinch of salt
1 tablespoon butter, melted
1 teaspoon white vinegar
1 cup milk

Sauce

1 cup double cream
175g (6 oz) butter
1 cup caster sugar
1 cup hot water

Have ready a 20 cm (8 in) round oven-proof dish, preferably Pyrex, and a piece of foil to cover it. Meanwhile pre-heat the oven to 180°C/350°F/Gas 4.

Using an electric whisk beat the egg, sugar and jam together until it is thick and pale. Sift the flour, bicarbonate of soda and salt together into a bowl. Now mix in one third of the milk to the egg mixture then one third of the flour. Continue to alternate them until all the milk and flour has been added.

Using another small bowl mix the butter and vinegar together. Add to the pudding mixture mixing well to combine. Pour into the dish. Cover with foil and seal the edges well. Bake in the oven for 45 minutes to 1 hour. The pudding is cooked when the surface is a consistent rich brown colour. If it is still too pale on top in the centre, continue to bake for a little longer.

While the pudding is baking, place all the ingredients for the sauce together in a pan and heat gently to melt the butter and dissolve the sugar. Re-heat and pour the sauce over the pudding as it comes out of the oven and serve hot.

If you are re-heating the pudding and it is slightly dry, pour over a little boiling water.

Banana Maple Pudding

Anne Wilkinson
Christchurch Council

Serves 6

<u>Topping</u>

> 30g (1 oz) butter
> 4 tablespoons maple syrup
> 2 ripe bananas

<u>Sponge</u>

> 115g (4 oz) butter beaten to soften
> 115g (4 oz) soft dark brown sugar
> 175g (6 oz) self raising flour
> 2 medium eggs, beaten.

Have ready an 18 cm (7 in) round shallow baking tin.
Pre-heat the oven to 180°C/350°F/Gas 4.

Prepare the topping: Put the butter and maple syrup into the baking tin and place in the oven for 5 minutes to mix and mingle. Meanwhile slice the bananas into approximately 1 cm (½ in). Remove the tin from the oven and stir the banana slices into the syrup mixture to coat them well. With the spoon push them into a single layer on the base of the tin.

To make the sponge: Cream the butter and sugar together. Mix in 1 tablespoon of the flour. Add all the egg a little at a time. Fold in the remaining flour. Pour the sponge mixture over the bananas. Place the tin in the oven to bake for 45 minutes until golden brown on top and risen.

To remove from the tin: Run a knife around the edge to loosen the pudding then invert the serving plate on top. Quickly turn them over and remove the tin. The pudding will come out onto the plate banana side up.

Delicious served with rum and raisin or coffee ice cream.

SORBETS

If you don't have a sorbetière or ice cream maker you can obtain good results using the freezer, but you must be prepared to take extra time.

Place the mixture into a bowl or container, and freeze for 1- 2 hours until semi-frozen. Whisk well and return to the freezer. Remove and whisk from time to time to break down large ice crystals, repeating until smooth and set.

Always chill your sorbet mixtures before making them by hand or using a machine, to retain the cold temperature of your freezer or machine for efficient use.

Pineapple and Malibu Sorbet

Gary Webster
Manor Arms

Serves 6 – 8

1 very ripe medium pineapple, peeled and chopped
OR
1 x 400g (14 oz) tin cubed pineapple
2 tablespoons water
Juice of ½ lemon
75g (2½ oz) caster sugar
A pinch of cinnamon
1 x 400ml (14 fl oz) can of coconut milk
1 tablespoon Malibu (or white rum or Bacardi)

Place the pineapple into a food processor.

In a small pan warm the water, lemon juice, sugar and cinnamon. Stir to dissolve the sugar then bring to the boil. Remove the pan from the heat and pour the syrup onto the pineapple.

Process to a smooth purée then pass through a fine sieve. Chill to refrigerator temperature.

Pour the mixture into a sorbetière or ice cream maker and churn for 15 minutes. Add the coconut milk and Malibu then churn until almost set, i.e. firm, smooth and with no large ice crystals.

Chocolate and Raisin Sorbet

Gary Webster
Manor Arms

Serves 6 – 8

500ml (17 fl oz) water
300g (9½ oz) caster sugar
125g (4 oz) cocoa powder (unsweetened)
75g (2½ oz) raisins, soaked in a light sprinkling of whisky.

5 teaspoons vanilla essence
1 tablespoon dark rum

In a medium pan mix the water, sugar and cocoa powder, place on a low heat and stir to dissolve the sugar. Then, on a high heat, bring to the boil. Remove from the hob, stir in the vanilla essence and rum then chill to refrigerator temperature.

Pour the mixture into a sorbetière or ice cream maker and churn for 20 - 30 minutes until firm and smooth. Add the soaked raisins and churn for a further 5 minutes.

Calvados Sorbet

Serves 6 – 8

300g (9½ oz) caster sugar
500ml (17 fl oz) water
1 vanilla pod, split lengthways
Juice of 1½ lemons

A pinch of cinnamon
4 large egg whites
175ml (6 fl oz) Calvados

In a small pan, warm the caster sugar, water and vanilla pod stirring to dissolve the sugar then bring to the boil. Remove from the hob and leave for 1 hour for the vanilla flavour to infuse into the syrup.

Strain the syrup into a medium bowl and discard the vanilla pods. Stir in the lemon juice and cinnamon. Chill to refrigerator temperature.

In a separate large bowl whisk the egg whites to a stiff peak and gently fold them into the flavoured mixture.

Pour into a sorbetière or ice cream maker and churn for 15 minutes. Add the Calvados and continue to churn until almost set, i.e. firm and smooth with no ice crystals.

Bakewell Tart

John and Sylvia Gray
Fredericks Restaurant, Highcliffe

Serves 4

115g (4 oz) short crust pastry
60g (2 oz) margarine or butter
60g (2 oz) caster sugar
60g (2 oz) ground rice
30g (1 oz) ground almonds
1 egg
2 tablespoons jam or lemon curd
Few drops of almond essence (optional)
3 tablespoons icing sugar
Blanched flaked almonds, to decorate
Glacé cherries, to decorate

Line a 18 cm (7 in) flan tin with the pastry, spread with the jam or lemon curd.

In a bowl, cream together the margarine or butter and sugar. Add the ground rice and the ground almonds to the mixture with the beaten egg and mix well.

Spread the mixture over the jam in the pastry case.

Bake in a pre-heated oven 190°C/375°F/Gas 5 for 40 - 45 minutes or until firm on top.

Allow to cool, then mix the icing sugar with a little water and spread over the top of the Bakewell tart, decorate with the flaked almonds and glacé cherries.

Banoffee Pie

Hilary Marshall
Red House Museum

Serves 4 - 6

Medium packet of digestive biscuits
Half a pack of butter
Tin of condensed milk
3 bananas
Carton of extra thick double cream
Cocoa powder or grated chocolate to decorate

Crush the digestive biscuits in a plastic bag using a rolling pin. Melt the butter in a saucepan and then add the digestive biscuits. Remove from the heat and stir until all the melted butter has been incorporated with the biscuit crumbs. Press the mixture into a flan dish and cool in the fridge.

Meanwhile take the tin of condensed milk and place in boiling water for three hours, check the water level to ensure that the tin remains covered with water. Remove and allow to completely cool.

Once cool, open the tin and spread the toffee mixture over the prepared biscuit base, cut the bananas into slices and spread over the toffee mixture.

Spread the carton of cream all over the top of the bananas. Serve as it is or decorated with either a sprinkling of cocoa powder or grated chocolate.

Whisky Bread and Butter Pudding

R.Chalmers, Head Chef
The Fishermans Haunt
Winkton, Christchurch

Serves 6 - 8

12 medium slices white bread
60g (2 oz) unsalted butter, softened
8 egg yolks
175g (6 oz) caster sugar
1 vanilla pod or a few drops of vanilla essence
300ml (10 fl oz) milk
50ml (2 fl oz) whisky
300ml (10 fl oz) double cream
30g (1 oz) sultanas
30g (1 oz) raisins
Additional caster sugar, to decorate

Grease a 1.75 litre (3 pint) pudding basin with butter.

Remove the crusts from the sliced bread and butter the bread. In another large bowl whisk together the egg yolks and caster sugar. Split the vanilla pod and place in a saucepan with the milk, whisky and cream. Bring this mixture to a simmer, then strain over the egg mixture, stirring all the time, to make a custard.

Layer the buttered bread in the prepared pudding basin sprinkling each layer with a few of the sultanas and raisins, finishing with a layer of bread. Pour the warm custard mixture over the bread, then allow to soak for about 20 minutes.

Pre-heat the oven to 180°C/350°F/Gas 4.

Place the pudding bowl in a roasting tin, three-quarters filled with warm water, and cook for 20 - 30 minutes until the pudding begins to set. Do not let it become too firm. Remove the pudding from the bain-marie and sprinkle liberally with caster sugar to cover the top.

Place under a medium grill to glaze the top allowing the sugar to caramelise.

You may find that the corners of the bread burn a little during this process, but this will add a wonderful bittersweet taste to the final dish.

Steamed Lemon Puddings with Raspberry Sauce

Mary Reader
Reader Communications

Serves 2

60g (2 oz) soft margarine
60g (2 oz) caster sugar
1 large egg, lightly beaten
60g (2 oz) self-raising flour
Zest and juice of ½ lemon

Raspberry Sauce

115g (4 oz) frozen raspberries, thawed
30g (1 oz) icing sugar
A few drops of lemon juice

Raspberries, blackcurrants to decorate

Grease two 150 ml (5 fl oz) ramekins or dariole moulds with a little oil or butter. In a large bowl, cream together the margarine and sugar. Add the egg, then fold in the flour. Add the lemon juice and zest. Divide the mixture between the two prepared ramekins and steam in a saucepan or steamer for 25 - 30 minutes. The pan should have 5 cm (2 in) of water in the bottom.

To make the sauce, drain and purée the fruit in a food processor or blender. Sieve the purée to remove the pips, then sweeten to taste with the icing sugar and add a few drops of lemon juice.

Once the puddings have cooked, remove from the ramekins and serve on a plate with the sauce poured over the top, decorate with the reserved raspberries and blackcurrants.

Strawberry Meringue Roulade
with Kiwi Coulis

A. Weir, Chef
Portfield School, Christchurch

Serves 10 - 12

8 eggs
450g (1 lb) caster sugar
900g (2 lb) strawberries
1.15 litre (2 pints) whipping cream
Strawberry melba sauce
450g (1 lb) granulated sugar
1.15 litre (2 pints) water
6 kiwi fruit

Grease a large 40 x 52 cm (16 x 20 in) shallow tray and line with greaseproof paper.

Separate the eggs and whisk the whites in a large (spotlessly clean) bowl until stiff, fold in the caster sugar and spread the mixture on the prepared tray.

Cook in a low oven 170°C/325°F/Gas 3 for 10 - 15 minutes until soft and chewy. Remove from the oven and turn onto greaseproof paper to allow to cool.

Wash and slice the strawberries and whip the cream.

Spread a little strawberry melba sauce over the cooled meringue, followed by the whipped cream and then the sliced strawberries. Roll up the prepared meringue and refrigerate.

To make the coulis, boil the granulated sugar with 2 pints of water until it starts to thicken, remove from the heat and allow to cool. Peel and chop the kiwi fruit, then purée the fruit and cooled sugar syrup in a food processor or blender.

When required, slice the roulade in 2.5 cm (1 in) slices and pour the kiwi coulis around the edge of the plate.

Boozy Banana Cream Pancakes

Sally Waugh & Susan Tabor
Suzettes Pancake House, Christchurch

Serves 4

450ml (15 fl oz) pancake batter mixture
60g (2 oz) butter
30g (1 oz) demerara sugar
4 bananas
150ml (5 fl oz) whipping cream
100ml (3½ fl oz) Baileys or Irish cream liqueur
Icing sugar and mint leaves to decorate

Make four 25 cm (10 in) pancakes. Pile them up, separating them with greaseproof paper, and keep them warm in a low temperature oven.

Slowly melt the butter in a pan, add the demerara sugar and heat gently until dissolved. Slice the bananas, reserving four slices for decoration, add to the mixture. Heat until the bananas are golden brown in colour and crisp.

Place the whipped cream and Baileys in another pan over a low heat. When the mixture comes to the boil, allow it to thicken slightly. Remove from the heat and add the caramelised bananas.

Remove the pancakes from the oven, divide the banana cream between the pancakes, creating a large triangular shape within the pancake. Fold in 2 sides to form a fan shape.

Place a banana slice at the point of the fan and top with a mint sprig. Sprinkle with icing sugar.

Serve with vanilla ice cream.

Rum Truffles

Joyce Lewis

Makes approximately 30

115g (4 oz) plain chocolate
60g (2 oz) butter
1 egg yolk, beaten
1 tablespoon apricot jam
1 tablespoon dark rum
175g (6 oz) icing sugar, sifted
115g (4 oz) digestive biscuits, crushed
60g (2 oz) raisins, chopped
Chocolate vermicelli, to coat

In a bowl, melt the chocolate with the butter over a pan of hot water. When melted, stir in the egg yolk. Remove the bowl from the heat and incorporate the jam, rum, icing sugar, biscuit crumbs and raisins. Mix thoroughly, then place the bowl in the fridge for at least ½ hour to allow the mixture to firm.

Remove from the fridge and roll the mixture into balls, using a teaspoon or melon baller, coat with the chocolate vermicelli.

Return the finished truffles to the fridge to completely harden.

Pineapple and Coconut Dessert Pie

The Boathouse,
Quomps Christchurch

8 tablespoons caster sugar
1 tablespoon margarine
2 egg yolks
12 tablespoons plain flour
1 cup milk
1 tablespoon baking powder

Filling

1 whole pineapple, peeled and crushed
2 cups caster sugar
5 cloves
1 stick of cinnamon
1 fresh coconut, grated
4 egg yolks

Beat sugar and margarine until pale white and creamy. Add the 2 egg yolks one at a time, beating well between additions. Add flour, milk and baking powder. Set to one side.

Cook the crushed pineapple, sugar, cloves and cinnamon for 5 minutes until the juices start to reduce, then add grated coconut and four egg yolks. Mix continuously until mixture comes together. Allow it to cool completely, then remove cloves and cinnamon.

Pre-heat the oven to 180°C/350°F/Gas 4.

Grease a square cake tin, divide the pastry in two and roll out to fit the tin. Put half the pastry in the tin and cover with the pineapple and coconut mixture. Cover with the remaining half of the pastry.

Bake in the oven for 50 - 60 minutes.

Serve warm with vanilla ice cream.

Honeycomb Mould

Linda Arnold
Red House Museum

This is a Georgian recipe for a pudding which is quite delicious. I make it often.

Serves 6

600ml (1 pint) full cream milk
3 eggs, separated
60g (2 oz) caster sugar
A few drops of vanilla essence
1 dessertspoon gelatine
2 tablespoons water
Small glass of mead
1 tablespoon runny honey

Put the milk in a saucepan and bring to the boil. Put the egg yolks and sugar into a bowl and pour on the milk, whisking continuously.

Pour the mixture back into the saucepan adding the vanilla essence and whisk over a low heat for a few minutes (do not allow to re-boil). Soak the gelatine in the water for a few minutes, heat gently until runny, then stir into the milk mixture. Add the mead and honey, stir well and then leave to cool for 15 minutes.

Whisk the egg whites until very stiff and fold into the cold custard.

Pour into a glass bowl or mould and chill until set.

Delicious on its own or served with puréed fruit.

Jellied Apple Mould

Linda Arnold
Red House Museum

450g (1 lb) cooking apples
150ml (5 fl oz) water
60g (2 oz) granulated sugar
1 packet of lime jelly

Peel, core and thinly slice the apples. Gently cook in a saucepan with the water and sugar until tender.

Remove from the heat, then whip the pulp with a fork until it is light, smooth and frothy. Cut the lime jelly into small pieces and add to the apple mixture.

When the jelly has been fully incorporated into the apple mixture, give a final whisk and then transfer to a jelly mould which has been rinsed with cold water.

Zabaglione

Antonio Maggio Carluccio
Pinocchio's, Christchurch

Serves 4

4 medium egg yolks
100g (3½ oz) caster sugar
170ml (6 fl oz) Moscato Passito

Beat the egg yolks with the sugar until the sugar is dissolved. Add the wine and beat for a few minutes more.

Put the bowl over a saucepan of gently simmering water and, using a whisk, beat until a firm, foamy consistency is obtained.

Pour the mixture into individual glasses and serve with delicately flavoured almond biscuits.

Apricot Cremé

Penny Baxter
on behalf of Winkton Residents Association

Serves 4 – 6

> 400g (14 oz) canned halved apricots, juice strained off
> 300ml (10 fl oz) double cream
> 300ml (10 fl oz) plain yoghurt
> 3 tablespoons soft brown sugar

Place the apricots singly cut side down in a glass bowl. In a mixing bowl whip the cream until it has thickened almost to peaking point. Stir in the yoghurt, and pour over the apricots.

Sprinkle with the brown sugar, cover with cling film and place in the refrigerator overnight.

*This recipe was also submitted by **Val Small**.*

Melting Moments

Joan Martin

Makes approximately 24

175g (6 oz) butter, softened
115g (4 oz) caster sugar, sifted
1 teaspoon vanilla essence
1 egg, separated
225g (8 oz) plain flour, sifted
A pinch of salt
45g (1½ oz) cornflakes, crushed

Lightly grease a baking sheet and pre-heat the oven to 190°C/375°F/Gas 5.

Put the butter, sugar, egg yolk and vanilla essence in a bowl and beat together until light and fluffy. Fold in the flour and salt and mix thoroughly.

Beat the egg white until frothy. Dip teaspoons of the mixture into the egg white, then dip into the crushed cornflakes until evenly coated.

Place them on the baking sheet and flatten into disc shapes with the bottom of a glass.

Cook in the oven for about 10 minutes until golden brown.

Cakes, Biscuits & Bread

In Edwardian times Taylor's Creamery occupied the large corner site at the junction of High Street and Castle Street. In the period between the two World Wars, Church Street acquired the nickname of 'Meringue Alley'. There were many tea shops in Church Street and neighbouring Castle Street at this time serving cakes and meringues filled with freshly whipped cream. Meringue shells were made at Hayballs bakery in Bargates.

Taking afternoon tea was a popular pastime and in the tea gardens locals and visitors alike could sit in the open air and enjoy their tea in pleasant surroundings. Newlyn and Ball ran Tuckton Tea Gardens in the 1920's. These gardens situated on the bank of the River Stour with views of the Priory and boat trips down the river to Christchurch Harbour and Mudeford Beach beyond are still there today.

Tea boats were also a common site in the harbour and one owned by the Derham family was moored off Avon Beach.

Ferry Tea Boat, Wick Ferry 1909

Whole Orange Spice Cake

Mary Berry

Serves 8 - 10

1 thin skinned orange
300g (10 oz) self raising flour
3 teaspoons baking powder
300g (10 oz) caster sugar
250g (8 oz) soft margarine
4 eggs
1 teaspoon ground cinnamon
1 teaspoon mixed spice

Icing

2 tablespoons orange pulp
60g (2 oz) soft butter
175g (6 oz) icing sugar, sieved

Pre-heat the oven to 180°C/350°F/Gas 4.

Grease and base line two 20 cm (8 in) sandwich tins with greased greaseproof paper.

Place the whole orange in a small saucepan, cover with boiling water and heat on a low heat until soft, about 1 hour.

When the orange is soft and cold, cut in half and remove any pips. Process the whole orange including the skin until medium chunky, reserve 2 tablespoons of the orange pulp for the icing. Add the remaining cake ingredients to the processor and blend until smooth, avoid over-mixing. Divide the mixture evenly between the tins.

Bake in the pre-heated oven for 20 - 25 minutes until golden brown.

Leave to cool in the tins for a few minutes then turn out, peel off the greaseproof paper and allow to cool completely on a wire rack.

To make the icing: Cream the soft butter, add the sieved icing sugar and reserved orange pulp. Sandwich the cakes together with icing, sprinkle the top of the cake with icing sugar.

To make the cake look extra special, scorch the top with hot skewers in a lattice design over the icing sugar.

Cheese and Apple Scofa Bread

Lesley Waters

A quick and easy instant bread. Serve warm with a bowl of warming winter soup.

Serves 8

250g (8 oz) self raising flour
½ teaspoon salt
2 eggs
125ml (4 fl oz) milk
4 tablespoons natural yoghurt
1 medium dessert apple, cored and finely diced
115g (4 oz) mature cheddar, grated
2 tablespoons chives, freshly chopped
Freshly ground black pepper

Pre-heat the oven to 200°C/400°F/Gas 6.

Lightly flour a non-stick baking tray.

Sift together the flour and salt. Season well with black pepper. In a separate bowl, beat together the eggs, milk and yoghurt. Stir the apples, cheese and chives into the flour.

Quickly and briefly, stir the wet ingredients into the dry ingredients. Turn the wet dough onto the prepared baking tray and form into a rough round. Mark with knife into 8 wedges and bake for 20 - 25 minutes.

To serve, break into wedges and serve warm.

Almond Slice

Natalie Gill

Excellent served with cream, ice cream or fromage frais.
Also ideal with a cup of tea or coffee.

Serves 6 – 8 square portions or approximately 16 "fingers"

225g (8 oz) made shortcrust pastry
115g (4 oz) caster sugar
115g (4 oz) icing sugar
115g (4 oz) ground almonds
60g (2 oz) semolina
2 eggs, beaten
2 teaspoons almond essence
60g (2 oz) flaked almonds
3-4 tablespoons raspberry jam

Have ready a baking tray 30 cm x 20 cm x 2 cm deep (12 in x 8 in x 1 in deep).
Pre-heat the oven to 200°C/400°F/Gas 6.

Roll out the pastry and line the baking tray with it. Lightly beat the jam to soften it and spread a light layer over the pastry base, refrigerate.

Meanwhile, sift the caster sugar, icing sugar, ground almonds and semolina into a bowl and stir lightly to combine. Beat in the eggs and almond essence. Continue until all are well mixed together.

Spread the almond mixture evenly over the jam, then sprinkle the flaked almonds on top. Bake in the oven for 30 minutes.

Remove from the oven, cool slightly and cut into wide fingers or squares to serve.

Damp Almond Cake

Ann Hyde
Bookends Bookshop

Serves 8

115g (4 oz) butter at room temperature
165g (5½ oz) caster sugar
3 eggs, beaten
2 drops almond essence
100g (3½ oz) ground almonds
40g (1½ oz) plain flour, sifted
A little extra butter, melted, and flour
Caster sugar to dredge

Pre-heat the oven to 180°C/350°F/Gas 4.

Grease an 18 - 20 cm (7 - 8 in) sandwich tin with melted butter. Cut a disc of non-stick baking parchment to fit the base and place inside the tin. Grease again, then dust with flour and tap out the excess.

Cream the butter then slowly add the sugar, beating until almost white and very soft. Beat in the egg a quarter at a time, beating well between each addition, then add the almond essence. Finally stir in ground almonds and the flour and mix well.

Place into the prepared tin and bake in the oven for 35 to 40 minutes until golden brown and springy to the touch. Remove from the tin and cool on a wire rack.

Dust with caster sugar before serving.

Tea Cake

Ann Hyde
Bookends Bookshop

Serves 12 - 15 slices

225g (8 oz) dried fruit (sultanas, currants, raisins)
300ml (10 fl oz) tea
2 teacups self raising flour
1 teacup soft brown sugar
1 egg, beaten
A little melted butter

Soak the fruit in the tea overnight.

Pre-heat the oven to 170°C/325°F/Gas 3.

Brush a loaf tin, approximately 23 x 13 x 8 cm (9 x 5 x 3 in) or of 1.5 litre (2½ pint) capacity, with a little melted butter. Put in a piece of non-stick baking parchment cut to fit the base.

In a large bowl mix together the flour, sugar and egg. Add the fruit and tea mixture. Mix well.

Pour into the prepared tin and bake in the pre-heated oven for 1 - 1½ hours until firm to the light touch of a finger and when a skewer inserted into the centre comes out clean. Remove from the tin and cool on a wire rack.

Slice to serve. Butter if wished, although the teacake has a very moist texture of its own.

Apple Fruit Cake

Sue Randle
Christchurch Council

Serves 8

225g (8 oz) plain flour
1 level teaspoon ground cinnamon
1 level teaspoon bicarbonate of soda
½ level teaspoon ground mixed spice
½ level teaspoon ground ginger
145g (5 oz) soft margarine
175g (6 oz) soft brown sugar
2 eggs, beaten
250ml (8 fl oz) canned apple purée
Grated rind of 1 lemon
450g (1 lb) mixed dried fruit
60g (2 oz) glacé cherries, chopped
60g (2 oz) chopped almonds
30g (1 oz) flaked almonds

Line the base and side of an 18 cm (7 in) round cake tin with greaseproof paper or baking parchment. Pre-heat the oven to 150°C/300°F/Gas 2.

Sieve together the flour, cinnamon, bicarbonate of soda, mixed spice and ginger. Cream together the margarine and sugar until light then gradually beat in the egg. Add the sieved flour mixture alternately with the apple purée then stir in the lemon rind, mixed fruit, glacé cherries and chopped almonds. Place the mixture into the lined tin, sprinkle the surface with the flaked almonds and bake in the oven for 1½ hours or until a skewer inserted into the centre comes out clean. Cool on a wire rack.

This cake may be frozen successfully.

Irresistible Mallow

Marion Paris
Christchurch Council

Makes 20 - 30 pieces

> 60g (2 oz) tiny marshmallows
> 115g (4 oz) hard margarine
> 450g (1 lb) digestive biscuits, crushed
> 1 tablespoon drinking chocolate powder
> 2 tablespoons golden syrup
> 450g (1 lb) Cadbury's milk chocolate or milk chocolate for cooking

Line a Swiss roll tin approximately 18 cm x 28 cm (7 x 11 in) with aluminium foil, then lightly oil the foil. Have a bowl of cold water ready and using scissors cut up the marshmallows into very tiny pieces, dipping the scissors into the water frequently to help prevent sticking.

In a medium sized pan add the margarine with the drinking chocolate and golden syrup and melt over a low heat. Remove from the heat and cool a little. Stir in the crushed biscuits and then the marshmallow pieces. Turn out into the prepared tin and with the back of a spoon press the mixture into the corners and smooth the surface.

Chill in the refrigerator until set. Cut up the chocolate roughly and place into a bowl. Melt it in a microwave or over a pan of steaming water. Ensure the base of the bowl does not touch the water. Spread the chocolate over the crumb mixture and replace the tin in the refrigerator until the chocolate has set. Cut into squares.

These may be keep in an airtight container, in a cool place, for some time.

Banana Loaf

Debbie Edlund

Serves 6

1¾ cups self raising flour
½ teaspoon bicarbonate of soda
½ teaspoon baking powder
¼ teaspoon salt
½ cup caster sugar
2 eggs
¼ cup milk
2 tablespoons butter or margarine, melted
1 cup mashed banana

Pre-heat the oven to 180°C/350°F/Gas 4.

Sift the flour, soda, baking powder, sugar and salt into a mixing bowl. In a separate bowl, beat the eggs then stir in the milk, butter and banana. Mix quickly into the dry ingredients, stirring until just combined.

Spoon into a greased loaf tin. Bake for 45 - 55 minutes, until a knife or skewer comes out clean from the centre of the loaf. Cool and serve.

Opposite: *Millefeuille of Winter Fruits with Champagne Syllabub (see p.126)*
Next page: *Carrot Cake with Walnuts and Mascarpone (see p.171)*

Summer Fruit Cake

Lillian Jeffries

175g (6 oz) butter
175g (6 oz) caster sugar
3 eggs
130g (4½ oz) self-raising flour
130g (4½ oz) plain flour
60g (2 oz) glacé cherries, chopped
225g (8 oz) mixed dried fruit
Grated rind of ½ lemon
2 tablespoons lemon juice
1 tablespoon demerara sugar

Pre-heat the oven to 170°C/325°F/Gas 3.
Grease and line a 18 cm (7 in) cake tin.

In a large bowl, cream the butter and caster sugar together.
Beat in the eggs gradually. In a separate bowl, mix the two kinds of flour, the cherries and the dried fruit. Fold the dry ingredients into the creamed mixture adding the lemon rind and juice. Mix well.

Pour the mixture in the prepared tin, spreading it evenly. Smooth the top and sprinkle it with the demerara sugar. Bake in the centre of the oven for 1¾ hours or until firm.

Previous page: *Glazed Date and Walnut Loaf (see p.178)*
Opposite: *Christchurch Priory from the Red House Museum*

Seasonal Biscuits

Jane Martin

115g (4 oz) margarine or butter
60g (2 oz) caster sugar
175g (6 oz) plain flour
A pinch of mixed spice (optional)
100g (3½ oz) icing sugar
5-6 teaspoons water

Icing pens
Biscuit cutters

Cream together the margarine/butter and caster sugar. In a separate bowl, sieve together the spice and flour and add it to the margarine and sugar mixture a little at a time and mix well until the dough forms a soft ball.

Roll out the ball on a lightly floured surface until it is about 5 mm (¼ in) thick.

Cut out desired shapes, e.g. angels for Christmas, eggs for Easter, ghosts or witches for Halloween. Place them on a greased baking tray and chill in the refrigerator for about 15 minutes.

Pre-heat the oven to 150°C/300°F/Gas 2.

Bake in the oven for 10 minutes or until golden brown. Cool on a wire rack.

Mix together the icing sugar and water until smooth. Spoon some icing on each biscuit and carefully level off with a knife. Leave to set.

Decorate further with icing pens if so desired.

Carrot Cake with Walnuts and Mascarpone

Mary Reader
Reader Communications

Serves 6 - 8

225g (8 oz) soft margarine
225g (8 oz) soft light brown sugar
4 eggs, beaten
275g (10 oz) self raising flour
2 teaspoons ground cinnamon
½ teaspoon salt
350g (12 oz) carrots, peeled and grated
85g (3 oz) walnuts, chopped

Filling and Topping

225g (8 oz) mascarpone cheese
115g (4 oz) ricotta cheese
60g (2 oz) icing sugar
6 halved walnuts

Prepare a 20 cm (8 in) deep round cake tin with a disc of greaseproof or silicone paper. Pre-heat the oven to 180°C/350°F/Gas 4.

In a large bowl or food mixer, cream together the margarine, sugar, eggs, flour, cinnamon and salt. Beat well for a minute. Stir in the carrots and chopped walnuts. Turn the mixture into the prepared tin and cook in the middle of the oven for 1¼ - 1½ hours. The cake is cooked when a skewer inserted in the middle of the cake comes out clean. If the top of the cake begins to look a little too brown before it is completely baked, lay a piece of foil lightly over the surface and continue baking.

Once cooked, leave the cake in the tin for 10 minutes. Remove from the tin and peel off the base paper, allowing the cake to cool for at least 2 hours before filling.

To make the filling and topping: In a medium sized bowl, mix the mascarpone and ricotta together. Add the icing sugar a little at a time mixing well.

Cut the cake in half horizontally, spread half of the cheese mixture on one cut surface and sandwich the cake together. Spread the remaining cheese mixture on the top of the cake and decorate with the halved walnuts.

Chocolate Brandy Cake

Somerford Junior School

Serves 6

115g (4 oz) butter at room temperature
2 tablespoons golden syrup
225g (8 oz) plain chocolate
175g (6 oz) digestive biscuits

115g (4 oz) walnuts
115g (4 oz) glacé cherries
1 tablespoon brandy

Melt the butter and the syrup together in a pan. Melt the chocolate separately over a pan of hot water.

In a bowl, break the digestive biscuits into rough pieces (do not crush) and add the walnuts and cherries. Stir the dry ingredients into the syrup mixture, then stir in the melted chocolate. Add the brandy and mix well.

Pour into a loaf tin or china bowl and chill well. Serve with cream.

Aussie Date Balls

Serves 6

175g (6 oz) caster sugar
½ teaspoon vanilla essence
1 egg
225g (8 oz) dates, chopped

145g (5 oz) margarine
2½ cups of Rice Krispies
½ cup desiccated coconut

Put the sugar, vanilla and egg in a saucepan, heat until combined. Add the chopped dates and margarine. Bring to the boil over a medium heat stirring all the time. Continue to boil for about three minutes until the dates are soft.

Allow to cool, then mix in the rice krispies. Form teaspoon size balls of the mixture and roll in the coconut.

Place on a greased baking tray and put in the fridge to set completely.

Sugar Free Fruit Cake

Gaynor
Salads Restaurant, Christchurch

Serves 8 - 10

175g (6 oz) wholemeal self raising flour
115g (4 oz) sunflower margarine
2 medium eggs
225g (8 oz) mixed fruit
115g (4 oz) chopped dates
30g (1 oz) desiccated coconut
½ teaspoon ground cinnamon
2 teaspoons vanilla essence
175ml (6 fl oz) cold water

Pre-heat the oven to 170°C/325°F/Gas 3.

Combine all the ingredients in a food mixer on a slow speed.

Grease and line a 1½ lb loaf tin. Place the mixture in the loaf tin and bake in the centre of the oven for 1¼ hours. Check the cake after an hours cooking.

Leave to cool in the tin completely then turn out onto a wire rack.

The cake may be kept in the fridge. It also freezes well.

One Cup Cookies

Rose Philpotts

Makes approximately 12 cookies

115g (4 oz) margarine, beat to soft
1 cup Alpen original muesli
1 cup self-raising flour
1 cup light muscavado sugar
1 size 3 egg, beaten
Ground nuts or desiccated coconut for coating

Have ready a greased baking tray or mince pie tin.

Pre-heat the oven to 160°C/315°F/Gas 2-3.

Mix all the cookie ingredients together, then roll the mixture into balls about the size of a walnut and coat each one with ground nuts or coconut.

Place them on the prepared tray well apart, leaving room for them to spread. Bake in the oven 15 - 20 minutes.

Short Cake

Makes 16 cakes

145g (5 oz) margarine or butter, at room temperature
85g (3 oz) caster sugar
225g (8 oz) plain flour, sifted
½ an egg, beaten

Cream the margarine until soft, slowly add the sugar beating until light and creamy. Beat in the egg then fold in the flour.

Wrap and chill 10 - 15 minutes, until firm enough to roll.

Cut the dough into 2 rounds and roll each flat and large enough to place into the base of a 18 cm (7 in) loose-bottomed sandwich tin, crimp the edges and mark each with a knife into 8 sections.

Chill, while pre-heating the oven to 200°C/400°F/Gas 6 then bake in the oven for 30 minutes to pale golden brown.

Shirley's Nutty Biscuits

115g (4 oz) margarine
1 cup caster sugar
1 cup self-raising flour
1 cup rolled oats
2 teaspoons golden syrup
1½ teaspoons boiling water
½ teaspoon vanilla essence
½ teaspoon bicarbonate of soda
A pinch of salt

Pre-heat the oven to 180°C/350°F/Gas 4.

In a large bowl, combine all the dry ingredients. Add the syrup, boiling water and vanilla essence and mix well.

Roll the mixture into 5 cm (2 in) balls and place on a greased baking tray, spaced well apart. Flatten the tops of the biscuits and bake in the oven for about 20 minutes until light brown.

Allow to cool slightly, then remove to a wire rack to cool completely.

Note : "Nutty" refers to the overall taste rather than any ingredient.

Cheese & Bacon Muffins

Elizabeth Richardson

Makes 6 - 8 muffins

115g (4 oz) fine cornmeal
145g (5 oz) plain flour
4 teaspoons baking powder
2 tablespoons light muscovado sugar
½ teaspoon salt
60g (2 oz) cooked bacon, chopped
115g (4 oz) mature Cheddar cheese, grated
1 egg, beaten
175ml (6 fl oz) milk
85g (3 oz) butter, melted

Pre-heat the oven to 200°C/400°F/Gas 6.

Butter a large 6 hole or medium 8 hole muffin tin.

In a large bowl, combine the cornmeal, flour, baking powder, sugar, salt, bacon and all but 30g (1 oz) of the cheese. In a small bowl, mix together the egg, milk and melted butter.

Add the egg mix to the cornmeal mixture all at once and stir until just combined and fairly stiff, do not over-mix. Spoon the batter into the muffin tin generously. Sprinkle over the remaining cheese.

Bake for 20 - 25 minutes until risen and golden. Leave in the tin for a few minutes, then transfer the muffins to a wire rack to cool.

Note: Cornmeal does not give a good rise when baking, so it is best to fill the tins to give a generous muffin.

Flapjacks

Michael Stannard

Makes 20 flapjacks

> 115g (4 oz) soft margarine
> 85g (3 oz) demerara sugar
> 2 heaped tablespoons golden syrup
> 225g (8 oz) rolled oats
> Large pinch of salt

Pre-heat the oven to 170°C/325°F/Gas 3.
Grease a 18 x 28 cm (7 x 11 in) rectangular shallow baking tray.

In a bowl, mix the margarine, sugar, golden syrup. Add the rolled oats and salt and mix together thoroughly.

Turn the mixture onto the prepared tray and press down and smooth with the back of a fork. Cut the mixture into fingers and cook in the centre of the oven for about 20 minutes until the flapjacks are golden brown. Do not over cook, or the flapjacks will become too crisp and brittle.

When cooked, cut around the inside of the tin and along the lines marking out the fingers. Allow to cool in the tin for about ten minutes then lift the fingers out with a slice and leave them on a foil covered wire rack to finish cooling.

Note : A non-stick baking tray is not suitable for this recipe.

Glazed Date and Walnut Loaf

Mary Reader
Reader Communications

Serves 6 - 8

175g (6 oz) self raising flour
30g (1 oz) soft light brown sugar
30g (1 oz) walnuts, chopped
30g (1 oz) stoned dates, chopped
30g (1 oz) soft margarine
1 tablespoon golden syrup
1 teaspoon lemon juice
2 eggs, beaten

Filling and Topping

1 tablespoon apricot jam
A few glacé cherries
Glacé apricots
2 dates
30g (1 oz) walnut halves
30g (1 oz) icing sugar

Grease a 450g (1 lb) loaf tin. Pre-heat the oven to 170°C/325°F/Gas 3.

In a large bowl put the flour, sugar, walnuts and dates.

Melt the margarine and golden syrup together in a small pan. Remove from the heat and then add the lemon juice. Leave to cool, then pour into the centre of the flour mixture and add the eggs. Mix to a smooth soft mixture. Pour into the prepared tin and bake for about 40 minutes. Remove and turn out onto a cooling rack.

To make the topping: Heat the jam with a little warm water in a small bowl. Brush over the top of the loaf and arrange the glacé fruits down the centre. Stone and halve the dates and arrange with walnuts on either side. Blend the icing sugar with a teaspoon of water and trickle over the top of the cake to give a criss-cross effect.

Dorset Apple Cake

A traditional recipe

225g (8 oz) self raising flour
115g (4 oz) butter
1 teaspoon mixed spice
600g (1 lb) cooking apples, peeled, cored and sliced
115g (4 oz) brown sugar
85g (3 oz) sultanas
2 eggs, beaten

Pre-heat the oven to 200°C/400°F/Gas 6.

Rub the flour and butter together in a large mixing bowl, add the mixed spice, sugar, apple slices, sultanas and egg. Mix together well.

Put the mixture into a large 25 cm (10 in) round cake tin.

Bake in the oven for 35 - 45 minutes.

Remove from the oven and allow the cake to cool for a few minutes before trying to remove the cake from the tin.

Jams, Sauces & Relishes

People have always used fruits and berries picked locally in their cooking in jam, wine and sauce making, in flavouring vinegar and for medicinal purposes.

Blackberries are perhaps the most popular 'free' fruit today because they are so versatile. Other berries such as sloes, rose-hips, red and blackcurrants are not used so much in cooking these days although redcurrant jelly is a traditional accompaniment to venison and other meats.

The microwave has made cooking jams much easier, less messy and time consuming than previously. The availability of good quality and exotic fruits has promoted renewed interest in this aspect of cooking.

Similarly travelling abroad has widened our experience of foods and one trend of the late 20th century has been to explore different combinations of tastes. This can be seen from the recipes for different sauces.

Newlyn & Ball Tea Gardens, Tuckton 1920's

MICROWAVE PRESERVES

Small quantities are easy and quick to make using the microwave. Always use a large bowl to allow for bubbling up without boiling over and keep fingers away from these very hot mixtures.

To test for setting point, have a well chilled small plate ready and spoon on a little of the mixture. Leave to cool for a few moments, then push a finger through the preserve. A skin should wrinkle in front of your finger and a light trail of visible plate should show behind it where the mixture does not immediately close over producing a spreadable, but not runny, jam.

Microwave Damson Jam

Susan Eckstein

Yields 2 - 3 x 350g (12 oz) jars

    600g (20 oz) damsons
    3 tablespoons water
    250g (8 oz) granulated or preserving sugar

Wash the damsons and remove the stalks. Place the damsons into a 3 litre (5 pint) mixing bowl with the water. Cook uncovered in the microwave on full power to soften the fruit. Remove the bowl from the microwave, add the sugar and stir to dissolve it. Return it to the microwave and cook on high for 6 minutes.

Remove the bowl and stir the contents to break the fruit and to free the damson stones. Skim off and lift out the stones and discard them.

Replace the bowl in the microwave and cook on full power for a further 6-8 minutes or until at setting point.

Cool slightly and put into clean, warm jars and seal while hot.

Microwave Raspberry Jam

Susan Eckstein

Yields approx. 3 x 350g (12 oz) jars

500g (1 lb) raspberries
½ teaspoon lemon juice
500g (1 lb) granulated or preserving sugar

Wash the raspberries, drain them and place them in a 3 litre (5 pint) mixing bowl. Microwave uncovered on full power for 5 minutes to soften them. Add the lemon juice and sugar, stir well to dissolve the sugar.

Return the bowl to the microwave and cook on full power for 15 minutes or until at setting point.

Cool slightly, pour into clean, warm, dry jars and seal while hot.

Red Onion Marmalade

The Boathouse
Quomps, Christchurch

1 kg (2½ lb) red onions, thinly sliced
2 tablespoons olive oil
½ cup brown sugar
Salt and freshly ground pepper

In a large pan, sauté the onions in the olive oil over a medium heat for 10 minutes. Season with salt and pepper, add the sugar and continue to cook over a low heat for a further 20 minutes, stirring. Taste and re-season if necessary.

Use as a garnish for prawns or goujons of fish.

Pernod and Grain Mustard Sauce

250ml (8 fl oz) dry white wine
250ml (8 fl oz) fish stock
1 tablespoon grain mustard
1 tablespoon Pernod
500ml (16 fl oz) double cream

In a pan, cook the wine and stock allowing to reduce away until it is almost gone. Add the mustard, Pernod and cream and cook for about 3 - 4 minutes until the sauce will coat the back of a spoon.

Use as a sauce for fish.

Variation: Replace the fish stock with veal stock for a sauce to accompany pork.

Fresh Courgette Chutney

Susan Eckstein

An excellent accompaniment to grilled, fried or roasted salmon with mashed or boiled potatoes.

Serves 4 - 6

1 tablespoon oil
1 medium onion, peeled and chopped
1 clove garlic, crushed
375g (12 oz) courgettes, thinly sliced
1 dessert apple, peeled, cored and roughly chopped
2 medium tomatoes, peeled, seeded and roughly chopped
1 tablespoon tomato purée
1 tablespoon white wine vinegar or cider vinegar
½ teaspoon chopped fresh tarragon
55g (1¾ oz) soft brown sugar
1 tablespoon dark soy sauce
A few drops lime or lemon juice
Salt and freshly ground black pepper
1 teaspoon chopped fresh coriander

In a large pan heat the oil, add the onion, cover and cook on a low heat until the onion is soft and translucent. Remove the lid, add the garlic and cook for 1 minute.

Add the courgettes, apple, tomato and tomato purée and cook on a high heat for 2 minutes. Pour on the vinegar and add the tarragon, simmer for 4 minutes.

Stir in the sugar and soy sauce, adding lime or lemon juice, salt and pepper to your taste.

To serve, re-heat until warm and add coriander just before serving.

Gooseberry and Dill Sauce

Susan Eckstein

An unusual, but traditional sauce to serve with Dorset mackerel, grilled whole to crisp and golden.

Serves 4

45g (1½ oz) caster sugar
3 tablespoons water
250g (8 oz) green gooseberries
 topped and tailed

1 tablespoon dill
30g (1 oz) butter
 cut into small pieces (optional)

In a medium pan place the sugar and water over a low heat and stir to dissolve the sugar. Bring to the boil and simmer for 1 minute. Add the gooseberries, cover and simmer until they are soft. Pour the mixture into a clean pan, re-heat and if using butter beat in a little at a time. Stir in the dill and taste, adding a little more sugar if necessary.

Variation: This is also very good served with roasted or grilled Dorset lamb, but leave out the dill. Add a small pinch of cinnamon or nutmeg to your taste for a change.

Apple and Ginger Chutney

Ann Hyde
Bookends Bookshop

Makes approximately 8 - 10 x 450g (1 lb jars)

3½ kg (7 lb) apples
500g (1 lb) onions
30g (1 oz) garlic
1.2 litre (2 pint) malt vinegar
1.5 kg (3 lb) soft brown sugar

1 teaspoon salt
1 teaspoon mixed spice
1 teaspoon Cayenne pepper
250g (8 oz) crystallised ginger
(finely chopped)

Peel, core and chop the apples, onion and garlic. Put them together in a preserving pan with 600 ml (1 pint) of the vinegar. Cook until all are soft. Add the spice, cayenne, salt, sugar, ginger and the remaining vinegar. Stir until boiling. Simmer for 15 minutes. Increase the heat and stir until thickened to a syrupy jam-like consistency. Put into warm jars and seal when cold. Keeps for ages, up to a year – if you don't eat it before!

Watercress Butter

Linda Arnold
Red House Museum

115g (4 oz) butter
1 small bunch of watercress
Salt and freshly milled pepper

Put the softened butter in a bowl. Remove and discard the coarse stalks from the watercress, wash and drain. Reserving one sprig, chop the remainder finely and combine with the butter, mixing thoroughly and seasoning with the salt and pepper.

Put in a serving dish and garnish with the reserved watercress sprig. Serve spread on bread or toast.

Tomato Butter

115g (4 oz) butter
1 tablespoon tomato purée
1 teaspoon tomato ketchup
A pinch of dry English mustard
A few drops of Worcestershire Sauce
Salt and freshly milled pepper
Slices of tomato and sprigs of parsley, to garnish

Put the softened butter in a bowl and beat in all the other ingredients, mixing thoroughly and seasoning with the salt and pepper.

Put in a serving dish and garnish with the slices of tomato and parsley. Serve spread on bread or toast.

Blackberry Vinegar

Simon Brickell

My Grandmother's tried and tested favourite remedy for colds and coughs.

450g (1 lb) blackberries
300ml (10 fl oz) plain (spirit) vinegar
1 tablespoon granulated sugar

Put the blackberries in a saucepan and pour in the vinegar, which should just cover the fruit. Bring to the boil and simmer briefly, add the sugar and continue to simmer for about 15 minutes until the blackberries are tender. When cooked, strain the liquid through a sieve and allow to cool. When cold, bottle and keep in the refrigerator or a cool place.

It should keep for at least six months.

Dose: Adults 2 - 3 teaspoons, 3 times a day
          Children (up to 12 years old) 1 teaspoon, 3 times a day.

Orange Honey

Linda Arnold
Red House Museum

450g (1 lb) granulated sugar
1 large orange
1 small teacup of water

Dissolve the sugar slowly in the water, then boil briskly for 10 minutes without stirring. Remove from the heat, add the juice and the finely grated rind of the orange. Allow to cool slightly, then stir with a wooden spoon until it becomes creamy. While it is still liquid, pour into a warm jar. It will set to the consistency of honey.

Shortcrust Pastry

Jane Lawley FIHEc
Head of Home Economics
Homefield School

225g (8 oz) plain flour
½ teaspoon salt
60g (2 oz) margarine and
60g (2 oz) white fat
or
115g (4 oz) butter
40ml (1½ fl oz) iced cold water (approx. 8 teaspoons)

In a large bowl, sieve the flour and salt together. Add the fat, cut into small pieces, and rub into the flour until the mixture resembles fine breadcrumbs. Add the water and mix to a firm dough. (This can be done in a food processor).

Turn onto a lightly floured surface, knead very gently until smooth. Continue until the underside and edges of the pastry are smooth and free from cracks.

Place the dough in a polythene bag or cover on a plate and refrigerate for 15 - 20 minutes before use.

Notes : Add the water slowly as it may be necessary to adjust the amount according to the quality of the flour.

Use butter in the pastry recipe for colour and flavour.

Microwave Pastry Case

Jane Lawley FIHEc
Head of Home Economics
Homefield School

1 quantity shortcrust pastry
1 egg yolk, beaten

On a lightly floured surface, roll out the pastry and use to line a 20 cm (8 in) Pyrex or microwaveable flan case.

Prick the base and sides of the lined case, then brush the pastry with the beaten egg to seal and give extra colour after cooking.

Bake the case "blind", using greaseproof paper and beans on full power for 3 minutes. Remove the paper and beans and microwave for a further 1 -2 minutes on full power.

If using a Pyrex dish, check through the base that the centre of the pastry should not be quite ready. This will allow for 5 minutes standing time during which the pastry will continue to cook.

Note: Times based on a 800w microwave

CONVERSION TABLES

Weights

oz	g
½ oz	15 g
1	30
1¼	40
1½	50
2	60
2½	75
3	85
4	115
5	145
6	175
7	200
8	225
9	250
10	280
12	350
14	400
1 lb	450
1¼	560
1½	675
2	900
3	1.4 kg
4	1.8
5	2.3

Volume

fl oz	ml
½ fl oz	15 ml
1	30
1¼	40
1½	50
3	90
4	125
5 (¼ pint)	150
10	300
15	450
1 pint	600
1¼	725
1½	850
1¾	1 Litre
2	1.15
2¼	1.3
2½	1.45
2¾	1.6
3	1.75
4	2.3

Measurements

inch	cm
¼ inch	0.5 cm
½	1
1	2.5
2	5
3	7.5
4	10
6	15
7	18
8	20.5
9	23
11	28
12	30.5

Oven Temp

Gas	°F	°C
Gas 1	275°F	140°C
2	300	150
3	325	170
4	350	180
5	375	190
6	400	200
7	425	220
8	450	230
9	475	240

Other

1 Teaspoon	5 ml
1 Tablespoon	15 ml
1 Cup	250 ml

Christchurch Cookery Book

Index

Index